The Best
of Bad
Hemingway

A HARVEST/HBJ ORIGINAL
HARCOURT
BRACE
JOVANOVICH

San Diego   New York   London

▼▼▼▼▼▼▼▼▼▼▼▼

The Best of Bad Hemingway

▼

CHOICE ENTRIES FROM THE
HARRY'S BAR & AMERICAN GRILL
IMITATION HEMINGWAY
COMPETITION

Introduction by
GEORGE PLIMPTON

▲▲▲▲▲▲▲▲▲▲▲▲

HBJ

Copyright © 1989 by Harry's Bar & American Grill
Introduction copyright © 1989 by George Plimpton

Special thanks to Mark Grody of Rowland Grody Tellem;
Marcia Abbott; and Sarah Peterson of Stanford University.

Library of Congress Cataloging-in-Publication Data
The best of bad Hemingway: choice entries from the Harry's Bar &
American Grill imitation Hemingway competition / introduction by
George Plimpton.—1st ed.
p. cm.
"A Harvest/HBJ book."
ISBN 0-15-611861-0
1. Parodies. 2. Hemingway, Ernest, 1899–1961—Parodies,
imitations, etc.
PN6149.P3B47 1989
818'.54'080351—dc19 88-26809

Designed by Michael Farmer & Joy Chu
Printed in the United States of America
First edition
A B C D E

As to Hemingway, I read him for the first time in the early forties, something about bells, balls, and bulls . . .

—*Vladimir Nabokov*

Contents

CONTENTS

CONTENTS

CONTENTS

CONTENTS

*Illustrations by Richard Thompson,
Mark D. Summers, Vint Lawrence,
Burges Green, Al Hirschfeld,
and David Levine appear on
pages 2, 24, 44, 64, 84,
and 112, respectively.*

INTRODUCTION

Then I turned and saw Gerty.
"Hello," she said.
"Hello," Ernie said.
"Hello," I said. . . .
"Tweedleboom and rumdum," Joyce said.
"Sit down down," Gertie said.
I sat down. Ernie sat down. We all sat down.

I have always admired this little parody—the skill of its author, Curtis H. Reider, managing to parody not only Hemingway, but also Gertrude Stein and James Joyce, all in the course of seven lines!

Of the three, one might think that Hemingway would be the most difficult to parody. After all, his principle was that a sentence should be so perfect, so superbly crafted that like an egg it would be hard to fault, much less imitate or poke fun at. And yet the attempt to write "the truest simple sentence that you know" ends up with such unique character that Hemingway is undoubtedly the most parodied American writer since Walt Whitman. I can recall examinations in comparative literature at college in which one was asked to identify the author of a body of unspecified text and explain why. It was always a relief to see a passage of Hemingway: it seemed to spring out of the page as if three-dimensional.

What is the Hemingway style? It is often typified by unlikely and imaginative juxtapositions. His correspondence in particular jostles with them, quite unreined, as if he were letting himself go just for the fun of it. Here's an example from a letter to Arthur Mizener in which the subject was his personal deity: "My God painted many wonderful pictures and wrote some very good books and fought Napoleon's rear-guard actions in the retreat from Moskova and fought on both sides at Gettysburg and did away with yellow fever and taught Picasso how to draw and sired Citation."

On the few occasions Hemingway talked about his writing style, he tended to dismiss its distinctive qualities as faulted rather than calculated. "In stating as fully as I could how things really were," he once told a group of young students, "it was often very difficult and I wrote awkwardly and the awkwardness is what they call my style."

What would Ernest Hemingway have made of this volume and its mimicry of his style? Probably not much. In his biography *Papa Hemingway*, A. E. Hotchner has an account of what Hemingway felt about E. B. White's spoof "Across the Street and into the Grill." Hemingway was not pleased. "The parody is the last refuge of the frustrated writer," he told Hotchner. "Parodies are what you write when you are associate editor of the Harvard *Lampoon*. The greater the work of literature, the easier the parody. The step up from writing parodies is writing on the wall above the urinal."

And yet, as all readers of Hemingway know, his second novel, *The Torrents of Spring*, was a savage parody of Sherwood Anderson, an early mentor who had given him letters of introduction to Gertrude Stein, Ezra Pound, and others when he went to Paris after the First World War. There are a number of theories about why Hemingway wrote it. Dwight Macdonald points out in the preface to his collection of parodies that the form is almost invariably written out of admiration rather than contempt. He poses the theory that Hemingway, who admired Anderson and acknowledged his debt, especially to the early stories, "had to kill the Freudian father in order to make his own place in the world of letters."

A more commonly held theory is that Hemingway dashed off the parody (he apparently finished it in seven days) in order to cancel his contractual obligations with the publishing firm of Boni and Liveright so he could move to Scribner's and its brilliant editor Maxwell Perkins.

Hemingway himself has offered a number of explanations. He often said he wrote *The Torrents of Spring* "to cool out" after finishing a draft of *The Sun Also Rises* and following a discussion with John Dos Passos about Anderson's novel *Dark Laughter*. A. E. Hotchner has a further amplification, which he either received in a letter or recorded, he could not remember which:

I wrote it because I was righteous which is the worst thing you can be. And I thought he was going to pot the way he was writing and that I could kid him out of it by showing him how awful it was. I wrote *The Torrents of Spring* to poke fun at him. It was cruel to do and it didn't do any good and he just wrote worse and worse. What the hell business of mine was it if he wanted to write badly. None. He had written good and then lost it. But then I was more righteous and more loyal to writing than to my friend. I would have shot anybody then, not killed him maybe, shot them just a little if I thought it would straighten them up and make them write right. Now I know there is nothing you can do about any writer ever. The seeds of their destruction are in them from the start. I'm sorry I threw at Anderson. It was cruel and I was a son of a bitch to do it. The only thing I can say is that I was as cruel to myself then, but that is no excuse.

What is clear is that Sherwood Anderson did not like what had been done. He suggested that *The Torrents of Spring* would have been better if Max Beerbohm, the master parodist, had taken the novel and cut it to ten pages.

Hemingway, by contrast, felt that Anderson had taken the whole matter in good humor. On January 12, 1927, he wrote Perkins: "Sherwood Anderson is in Paris and we had two fine afternoons together . . . He was not at all sore about 'Torrents' and we had a fine time." Anderson does not remember the "two fine afternoons." He describes Hemingway calling on him just as he was about to leave Paris:

There was a sudden knock on the door, and there Hemingway was.

He stood in the doorway.

"How about a drink," he said, and I followed him down a stairway and across a street.

We went onto a small bar.

"What will you have?"

"Beer."

"And you?"

"A beer."

"Well, here's how."

"Here's how."

He turned and walked rapidly away.

The Torrents of Spring was not well accepted critically when it appeared. Harry Hansen of the *New York World* wrote, "Parody is a gift of the Gods. Few are blessed with it. It missed Hemingway." That may be putting it too strongly. There are some genuinely clever scenes in *The Torrents of Spring*—in particular the takeoff on Anderson's sex-mysticism and his preoccupation with childish symbols. The hero, Scripps O'Neil, keeps a bird inside his shirt to which he feeds beans ("Beans for the bird!") and shows to young women he fancies. It is a curious conceit when one recalls that a bird often crops up in Hemingway's own sex scenes: the white bird that flutters out of the gondola in *Across the River and into the Trees* when Colonel Cantwell and the countess are making love, the owl flapping through the forest in the Nick Adams story.

I once had the temerity to ask Hemingway about those birds. We had just come back from a day's fishing on the Gulf Stream. He was in a fine mood. But the question infuriated him. "I suppose you can do better!" he shouted at me, which was a formidable comment to one whose only literary output up to that time was a children's book entitled *The Rabbit's Umbrella*!

It wasn't much fun to judge Hemingway. In the Finca Vigía living room he once sat me down in a large overstuffed chair and gave me a chapter in manuscript of *A Moveable Feast* to read. He crouched immediately behind the chair, following the text along with me, so that I was aware of his whiskered face, the whisper of his breath in my ear. When I would nervously laugh at something, he would instantly ask what it was that had amused me. I would point a wavering finger at the page, which would produce a kind of rumbling grunt from the back of his throat. I can hardly recall moments of more anguish—certainly not in the course of *reading*!

I must say the memory of that afternoon in the finca crossed my mind a number of times when I was asked to be a judge of the International Imitation Hemingway Competition, whose best entries are collected in this volume.

A word about the contests, which, alas, after eleven years have run their course: the first Hemingway competition took place in 1978, six years after Harry's Bar & American Grill, a replica of Harry's Bar in Florence, Italy, opened in Century City, adjacent to Beverly Hills. The competition was the brainchild of an advertising man named Paul Keye. He knew that Hemingway never went to the Harry's Bar in Florence but that his attachment to the original Harry's Bar in Venice was known worldwide. Mention of it turns up in *Across the River and into the Trees*:

The waiter made the call while the Colonel was in the bathroom.

"The contessa is not at home, my Colonel," he said.

"They believe you might find her at Harry's."

"You find everything on earth at Harry's."

"Yes, my Colonel. Except, perhaps, happiness."

"I'll damn well find happiness too," the Colonel answered him. "Happiness, as you know, is a moveable feast."

Paul Keye saw the obvious promotional value of attaching the Hemingway name to the Century City offshoot. Thus the competition. In his original advertising copy he noted that contestants would have to face "The White Bull That Is Paper With No Words On It." The only stipulation in the contest was that Harry's Bar had to be mentioned in the parody (and not disparagingly!). The application blanks asked for "a really good page of really bad Hemingway." Whoever was best at it was to be flown abroad (with a partner of his or her choice) and rewarded with a dinner at Harry's Bar in Florence. Once in Florence the winners were asked to make their own accommodations. "We feed you . . . and send you back. Okay?"

A lot of people thought this *was* okay because in the eleven years of the competition more than twenty-five thousand Hemingway parodies were received. Rarely has the saying "imitation is the sincerest form of flattery" been as truly exemplified.

Over the years the seven jurists who have taken "the bull by the horns"—as the quip goes—have included Jack

Hemingway, who stands midway between the fame of his father and his actress daughters; the novelist Ray Bradbury; Herb Caen of the *San Francisco Chronicle;* Barnaby Conrad, the novelist and bullfighting aficionado; Jack Smith, a *Los Angeles Times* columnist; Digby Diehl, a former *Los Angeles Herald Examiner* columnist; the San Francisco poet Lawrence Ferlinghetti; Joseph Wambaugh, the novelist; and Bernice Kert, the author of *The Hemingway Women,* who reputedly brought an increased sense of decorum to the proceedings. These worthies (and others over the years of the competition) met in either of California's Harry's Bars (there is now one in San Francisco) to pick over the twenty-odd entries winkled out of some 2,500 submissions by a group of preliminary readers. As Ray Bradbury once put it, "We were trying to separate the good bad Hemingway from the bad bad Hemingway." Occasionally there were major disagreements. One year the jury was deadlocked at three apiece (the seventh member had never turned up) until finally an excess of wine (so the story goes) knocked one of them into such senseless gibbering that his vote was discounted and a winner declared.

As mentioned, I was a judge for one of the earliest competitions. I remember a steady afternoon of reading. It was before the days of preliminary culling. The entries arrived at Harry's Bar in gray mail sacks. We worked behind mounds of manuscripts, reeling out into the night after seven hours or so. It was often laborious. The vast majority of the entries lacked the humor or wit that is so essential in first-rate parody. During a stretch of unrelenting reading, unrelieved by so much as a chuckle, one judge (I think

Digby Diehl) wondered aloud if it wasn't an imitation Sylvia Plath contest being assessed!

In the later years, with the entries screened by a panel of so-called "professional educators," the final selection took only an hour and a half and would have taken even less if not for Barnaby Conrad; he was famous among the jurists for being slow, largely because he accompanied his reading with a steady stream of comments. The others waited at the bar while he plowed slowly through the final selections.

When the judging was finally complete, Digby Diehl, apparently the ham among the judges, read the winning entry aloud, greeted with *olés* and napkin waving from the others as if he were performing in a bullring. In the latter years of the competition the media were inevitably on hand not only for this ceremony but for what preceded. It always astonished Diehl that a kind of involved joke attracted so much attention—that television crews from as far away as Germany would crowd into a tavern to focus their cameras on seven people sitting around a table *reading!*

I am told that the Hemingway competition has come to an end because it was too time-consuming. Management spent more time processing the enormous number of entries than running the restaurants. I wonder. How could one do away with such a splendid promotion? My own feeling is that someone in charge, working out the next year's program, suddenly became aware of a faint breathing behind the ear, perhaps the scratch of whiskers, and quickly reckoned, Well, quite so: enough is enough!

—*George Plimpton*

Across the Street and Street and into Harry's

▼

C H O I C E E N T R I E S F R O M
T H E C O M P E T I T I O N

Miss Stein instructs E. H. on how to develop his writing arm.

The Crullers

▶ ▶ ▶ ▶ ▶ *T*he door of Harry's Bar & American Grill opened and two men came in. They sat down at the bar.

"What's yours?" Harry asked them.

"Crullers," one of the men said. "We want crullers."

"I don't know if I want crullers," the second man said. "I don't know what I want to eat."

Outside it was getting dark. The two men at the bar read the menu.

"I'll have two crullers," the first man said.

"We don't serve crullers," Harry said.

"Why the hell do you call yourself an *American* bar and grill? Crullers are American. Americans eat crullers!"

"Not here they don't," Harry said. "This is Florence."

"Who the hell is Florence?" the second man said. "We're not interested in broads. We want crullers."

"Sorry," Harry said. "No crullers." He looked at the clock on the wall behind the bar.

"It's five o'clock," the first man said. "Time to start making the crullers."

"Don't know how," Harry said. "No call for them here."

"You're a pretty bright boy, aren't you?" the second man said. "You can figure out how to make crullers." He turned to the first man, "Can't he, Al?"

"He's dumb," Al said. "Too dumb to figure it out." Al pushed his derby hat back off his forehead. "Where's Oxenfree?" he said.

"You mean Olie Oxenfree?" Harry asked.

"Yeah, bright boy," the second man said. "Olie. Olie Oxenfree."

"Sometimes he comes here for dinner," Harry said. "What's it all about?"

"Crullers," Al said. "It's about crullers." His eyes were cold and he licked his lips. "Olie Oxenfree was the cruller king of Chicago. Then he mixed up a bad batch."

"Yeah," the second man said. "A bad cruller can kill you."

Harry reached down for a towel and wiped the bar. "Crullers can be cruel," he said.

"Well," Al said, "you'd better not think about it."

—*Corinne Latta*

THE SNOOZE OF KILIMANJARO

Kilimanjaro is a big mountain 19,410 feet high, and that's not counting the TV transmitter. The summit, marked by a single welcome mat, is called "Mmble-Brnxp," the Front Porch of God. Close to the summit are the frozen remains of a lemonade stand. No one has explained why anybody would try to sell lemonade at that altitude.

▶ ▶ ▶ ▶ ▶ *H*e had come with the woman to Kilimanjaro to gather ideas for a cycle of haikus he was writing. The woman had suggested, in the aristocratic manner of the rich, that living on a diet of dried bark and dirt would toughen something inside him that had gone soft and prevented him from creating. Instead it softened him further, and now he was dying of severe dysentery complicated by writer's block.

Now he would never write the things he had saved to write until he learned to spell them. For instance, "accommodation." One *C*, two *M*s, or the other way around? He wasn't sure. Or "chrysanthemum"? On rugged Kilimanjaro, there was not even a dictionary.

"How do they know I'm dying?" he asked the woman, pointing to the crowd of undertakers, florists and wake caterers who were gathering at the edge of the campsite. "Is it the odor?"

"Or your dysentery?" she asked. "Or your poetry?"

She knew how to hurt him, this woman, this female being, this person of the nonmale persuasion. And he would have hurt her back, at least challenged her to a thumb wrestle, if he hadn't felt it just then. The cold stale breath.

Death.

He could taste Death in the wind. He could hear it tiptoe around the campsite. He could see it climbing a tree, hiding in a garbage can, tripping over a root. Clumsy Death. Once he thought Death tapped him on the shoulder, but it must have ducked when he turned around to see who it was. "The night can play strange tricks on a man," the woman had said. Sure enough, when he awoke the next morning, there was a "Kick Me" sign pinned to his back.

Sensing Death nearby, he wished he had never left his comfortable job at Harry's Bar, where he had made good money as a cocktail waitress during a confused period of his adolescence. Yes, that was another story he would never write, mainly because he couldn't even pronounce *scampi grigliati*, let alone spell it. For him, there was but one haiku left to write.

> I came for ideas
> But instead I'm going to die
> You rotten mountain.

He scratched the words into the pile of uneaten dirt and waited for Death to stumble his way.

—Mark Silber

"ELENA. COME HERE,
MY LITTLE GERBIL . . ."

▶ ▶ ▶ ▶ ▶ "*E*lena. Come here, my little gerbil," Max Winchester said, and his arms were strong. He
knew he would be the first but he would teach her of love.
He saw her looking in fear of the lumpy form in a corner
of his room. "That is only old Primitivo, a man of the ages.
Just ignore him," Max said.

"Ah, *Inglés,* before the dew comes I must go. There are
rules here at the 'Y.'" She knelt and nibbled his femur.

"That is the femur," he said. "So little can be told of it."
He had a pack of Chesterfields in his hand and he knew,
and he saw her face above the tobacco stamp. She had no
pack of Chesterfields and that was only a part of what was
and what was not between them. Across the room Primitivo
sucked his teeth, as a certain kind of man will do.

"Ah, Max, you are a man. Let us do quickly the things
that we must."

"Stand, my little gerbil," Max Winchester said. "Stand
and come to me." Now as they stood and held and stood
and pressed and fell to the woven mat, suddenly a vein-
pulling lonely happiness filled him and he knew that the

time had come, it was called fate. "Tomorrow I will take you to Harry's," he said.

He knew that she felt the full meaning of those words.

"I am, then, your woman? You will take me to Harry's and perhaps we will share some *scampi grigliati* and the night will be new and we will be new and you will stay with me forever and we will have a blender and a Jacuzzi?"

A sunrise is sometimes a sunset. A man can be wrong about a woman.

"How do you know of the *scampi grigliati,*" he asked, and he heard her sob and he knew that she had already been to Harry's with a man.

"Yes, yes, *Inglés,* it's true, and now you will never want me and you will stay here with that old swine who mucks me with his eyes."

"Come, Primitivo," said Max Winchester. "Come with me to Harry's and we will share a liter of Chianti and we will speak of the men in blue shirts and of the women for whom we were the first and of the many years we worked together selling municipal bonds." He looked out the window. It was a sunset. He knew now that it was a sunset.

—*Patricia Traxler*

In the Late Summer of That Year
We Lived in a Condo

*I*n the late summer of that year we lived in a condo in North Dallas that looked across the tollway to the discos and honky-tonks of the rue St. Bubba. We were young and our happiness dazzled us with its strength. But there was also a terrible betrayal that lay within me like a Merle Haggard song at a French restaurant.

"The Great Landry says the Cowboys will be back," said the girl.

"Then it must be so," I said though I knew it was a lie.

"When football season comes, then it will be cold. Like Switzerland. But not now. The cold will be back later."

"Pass the Doritos," I said and her eyes shone like the stars over Amarillo.

I could not tell the girl about the woman of the tollway, of her milk-white BMW and her Jordache smile. There had been a fight. I had punched her boyfriend, who fought the mechanical bulls. Everyone told him, "You ride the bull, *señor*. You do not fight it." But he was lean and tough like a bad rib-eye and he fought the bull. And then he fought me. And when we finished there were no winners, just men doing what men must do. And the pain was washed away but the image of the woman stayed with me like a blessing and like a curse.

We went that summer to many clubs. We went to the Longhorn Ballroom and to the Palm and to a honky-tonk in Fort Worth that was what Harry's Bar would have been like if it had eighty-five–cent Pearl Beer and a barmaid whose peroxide hair could damage your eyes as if you had watched an eclipse. That night we visited them all, but as we drove home I did not think of the Pearl Beer and I did not think of the peroxide. I did not think of the girl who sat beside me. I thought of the woman of the tollway, and I could feel my heart pounding in the heat of the summer night.

"Stop the car," the girl said.

There was a look of great and terrible sadness in her eyes. She knew about the woman of the tollway. I knew not how. I started to speak, but she raised an arm and spoke with a quiet and peace I will never forget.

"I do not ask for whom's the tollway belle," she said. "The tollway belle's for thee."

The next morning our youth was a memory, and our happiness was a lie. Life is like a bad margarita with good tequila, I thought as I poured some whiskey onto my granola and faced a new day.

—*Peter Applebome*

José Was a Man of Size

*J*osé was a man of size. This is why he could laugh in such a large way when the bird sat on his cigar. José's cigar was the size of a monkey's arm. Because of the rain, José's large cigar would not light as he sat at a café table in the rain. The bird came tiny on the rain and sat on José's cigar at the café and José laughed.

"It is good," said José "that this bird has come tiny on the rain to sit at the end of my cigar that will not light."

For José knew with a fierce knowledge that the men who wanted him to go away with them would never come to sit here in front of Harry's Bar in the Florentine rain. No. They would only sit to laughter and good talk and good wine when the sun had also risen, risen to warm the air for the flying of the little birds that they would feed.

Knowing this, José could eat the *pasta al ultimo dente* that was prepared here, in this Florentine season of rain, as it could be prepared nowhere else. José knew he could hold the rain away with an umbrella while he put fork to pasta and this too was a fierce knowing in him, fierce and quiet and a little proud too.

While José ate and watched the bird on the end of his

sodden cigar and sipped Harry's good whiskey he thought about how they had taken Martin and George away, taken them away before they had even finished arguing about the death of the dromedary.

Everyone agreed that the dromedary had died well.

When José had finished it all, the pasta, the good whiskey, the thinking about George and Martin and the dromedary, he stood in the Florentine rain and walked away from Harry's. He watched him go and then we saw the tiny bird fly away. The bird was tiny and it could not carry a cigar the size of a monkey's arm. So the bird too had to go away in the rain carrying nothing. Then we came out of Harry's and put the table away in a dry place that Harry had and when the men came for José all they could see was the cigar. The cigar was very wet now and it was softening and changing in the rain in the gutter in front of Harry's.

The men could see that it was a fine cigar but Wet Cigars Cannot Be Smoked. The men argued about it, what it meant, and we all came out of Harry's to stand in the rain and listen to the men argue. Finally they agreed that sometimes a cigar is Just a Cigar but it was a fine, tough argument and the men went away to look for José in another place.

—*William D. Frank*

WOMEN WITH MEN

▶ ▶ ▶ ▶ ▶ "It is a beautiful day," said the woman, leaning out the window.

The man nodded his head. "It is well and truly beautiful."

The woman turned and smiled, then crossed the shabby hotel room and stood in front of him. "Today we should go for a drive in the country. Don't you think we should do that on such a beautiful day?"

"No," said the man. "I would like to kill something on a day like this. I would like to kill something swift and beautiful as it leaps through the air. I wish I had my rifle with me. I feel naked without my rifle."

"A real man wouldn't," said the woman.

"What do you mean by that?" said the man.

"I mean a real man could hunt without a rifle. Don't you remember Africa when you had dysentery and the porters were scared away by the lion and I had to wrestle it to the ground. I think I broke a nail. Didn't I break a nail then?"

"Don't talk to me about Africa. I do not like to talk about Africa."

"Let's talk about Michigan, then," said the woman. "It was a beautiful day like this when I had to kill that bear with a hatchet."

"Do not talk to me of Michigan," said the man. "I do not like to talk about Michigan. I should have known when I met you in Florence what sort of woman you were."

"I loved Florence," said the woman. "Remember when I drank you under the table at Harry's Bar?" The woman laughed in a high, feminine voice that crackled against the walls.

"Do not talk to me of Harry's Bar," said the man. "I do not like to talk about Harry's Bar."

"But we were always happiest at Harry's Bar, weren't we?"

"Yes, we were always happy at Harry's Bar."

"But do you remember when we got too drunk and had a fight?"

The man nodded his head and leaned back in his chair. "I remember. If I hadn't been distracted you never would have decked me."

"That's not true," said the woman. "I could always knock you flat."

"Not true."

The woman stared at the man. "Of course it's not true," she said. She walked over to the closet, opened the door, and fished out two pairs of boxing gloves as the man sat watching her silently.

"Here," she said, tossing one pair of mittens into his lap. "Prove it!"

—Greg Aunapu

IN ANOTHER CONTRA

▶ ▶ ▶ ▶ ▶ The man loved Harry's. He could always get what he needed at Harry's. Too bad Harry's Bar was a world away and he was wounded and weary and would walk no farther. The man was going to settle for the stinking seaside *bodega* and that was bad and he would hate himself later. He spat in disgust—carefully downwind, as the Patagonian gypsy had taught him—then he kicked in the front door.

The man, whose name was nondescript, unslung his *máquina* and placed it on the bartop, gently, as if it was asleep and he wished not to wake it. It was his favorite machine gun. They had been together for years. Men who knew of guns and subordinate clauses said that when the gun was fired, it leaped and twisted with the iridescent violence of a taildancing black marlin, yet it was not nearly so slimy.

"A good and fine weapon, *señor*. Who is its maker?" The barman reached for the gun but recoiled when it growled at him.

The man eyed his host warily, wondering if he took Visa. "My weapon is a Deus X, model 20."

"Ah, a Deus X *máquina*. A miraculous and convenient

device, eh?" The barman looked like a fat weasel, the man thought to himself. "*Sí,* many villains have been foiled, many conflicts resolved with one of these doozies, have they not, *señor?*"

"You've got a hell of a breath," the man replied. Be careful, the man said to himself. This *cabrón* speaks with a sadness you have heard before. It is badness. It is the sadness that comes before the big sell-out.

The barman smiled his weasel smile. "Perhaps you would like to buy my café, *señor?* For you, *nada* down. *Nada y nada* for six months and included are all the wild-game trophies on the walls. I ran them all over myself, and not with a filthy automatic transmission. All the sporting way, with stick shift."

The barman's words were lost as the café echoed with the sounds of killing. "This day is the worst," said the man. "The poor bastards keep dropping like flies."

"But *señor*, they are flies. It is the *mosca frita,* my bug zapper." The barman fought back his weasel tears. "They seek the light. That is their downfall."

"I seek the light also," said the man. "As long as it tastes great and is not too filling."

The two men in overcoats at the end of the bar scowled and fingered their violin cases. "Did you hear that, Al?" the one not named Al said. "We got ourselves a bright boy. He says he seeks the light, just like a real bright boy. Know what we do to bright boys?"

"Aw, don't get sore," said the man. "Finish your bevo and go easy on the repetitive wordplay. I have a headache already. I got it when I brought the little gorillas down to the beach to teach them manly things and instead the lousy wimps want to build sand castles!"

"Oh, *señor*," groaned the barman. "They will surely become the worst kind of *mocosos—Sandy Kneestas!*"

It was too late. They had found him and they came to him shrieking their horrible whining cries—"Uncle Murray, we're hungry!" "Uncle Murray, we're sunburned and we want to go home!" He felt the gun jump in his hands, the barrel climbing with each burst. It was an excellent watergun with new batteries and he was soaking them good. They tore at his ankles. He turned to the barman. "Will you help us?"

The answer came from under the bar. "Of course, *señor*. Take my Audi. Please."

—Dave Curtin and Diana Curtin

Arriba y Abajo

► ► ► ► ► *W*e were drinking at a bar in Irún watching the bartender and the bartender was leaning over his bar and saw us looking at him and he smiled. His name was Juan Dinero. He was young and dark and good-looking. He was a *novio*, a new bartender that year.

The drinking began at Harry's Bar & American Grill in Firenze and I suggested driving to Irún for the *Borrachera* and so we drove to Irún. *Borrachera* means the deep drinking. It is a ritual. It lasts many days. People come to drink and to see the new bartenders. There is music and noise and much drinking. It is a ritual and it lasts for many days.

Juan was working a *borracho*. *Borracho* means drunk. Juan worked his *borracho* smoothly and suavely, keeping him close, keeping him from counting his change, making him consent with his body to more and more of the drink. In the end the *borracho* would lie supine and his toes would curl and the ritual would be fulfilled.

I loved the bartending deeply. "You have *corazón*," someone told me. *Corazón* means heart. If you have heart you love the bartending deeply. You are a *corazonado*. If you are a *corazonado* people know you have the love for the great purity of the bartending.

In the bartending there is the terrain of the bartender and the terrain of the *borracho*. Juan worked the terrain of the *borracho*. The terrain of the *borracho* is the more difficult. Juan always leaned far over the bar and worked with absolute purity of line in unbroken glides that would not leave the *borracho* wasted or discomposed. I think Juan had the greatness.

I watched him twirling an eleventh Fundador over the head of the *borracho* and bringing it to rest in a single movement of grace and the eyes of the *borracho* never leaving the eyes of Juan and the *borracho* gulping the Fundador and sliding gently off his stool and lying with open eyes fixed on the ceiling. It was not great bartending. It was only perfect bartending.

"Muy borracho," Juan said. He flicked his bar towel as if waving a banner. *"Muy borracho,"* I said.

—*Walter N. Trenerry*

INTO THE RIVER AND UP TO YOUR KNEES

► ► ► ► ► *T*hat spring the Italians were very brave. They came across the river in red shorts waving passports and we shot them. It was later in Harry's Bar & American Grill. I saw how beastly war had been. It was the old thing. I had been up in Montana. Madrid had been a portable fiesta. But in Paris I had a Visa card. Brat came in from Gertrude's garage sale.

"Was it good?" I said.

"Rags," she said magnificently.

"What size?" I said.

"Go *obscenity* yourself," she said.

Brat had nice buns. They stuck out. She loved the bulls. She stole English raincoats, liked champagne, loafers, and punchy novelists. Suddenly everything was heroic, low-key, and overweight. After a Fleurie, I ordered pizza and we stopped at Le Cochon Littéraire for oysters, snails, frogs, and liver. Brat ate a moose. I ordered a drink:

"Pernod."

"We don't serve that *obscenity*," the barman said.

Then the barman said bad things. He knew he would die.

He was good. As he poured, his hands never left his body. He was damn good. I knew he would die.

"Hot chocolate," I said.

"And the *obscenity,*" the barman said.

"Give the lady another *château,*" I said.

It was good to be in Paris without a Guggenheim. Life felt very clean. Fitzy arrived in a suit. He was a poet. His cough was very bad. His bandages needed changing. He was cold. It was damn cold. I was okay.

"Nice suit," I said. I was lying.

"Garage sale," he said.

"L.A. is tough," I said.

"This is Paris," he said. He was a coward.

"Chocolate?" I said. We were poor. Damn poor.

"Naked existential women," he said.

After the Fleurie, the Pernod, the chocolate, some Sion wine, the antifascist's pizza, hot chestnuts, a dozen *moules,* and some wonderfully rotten cheese, I was sick. We dashed to the Two Worms to meet X. We talked a long time about X over a simple, excellent, slightly fashionable meal. Brat and I walked to the rue des Italiennes Mortes. I wasn't angry at Brat, Brat wasn't angry at me. It was raining like hell. I thought about my lunch, about my sperm count, and about the hole in the bullfighter at Pamplona and about having preppy intercourse before the rich came. Life was very clean.

"Cuddle?" said Brat.

"Go take a bath," I said.

That was Paris in spring. It felt very good thinking about food and writing and the bullfighter's hole. Life was semi-sacred if a man kept one hand in his pocket and smiled a lot. When the rains stopped I stayed good in the head and fondled my rabbit's foot. Despite the other thing we were very poor and very happy. I grew a moustache.

—*Philip Daughtry*

It Was Now Morning and He Was in the Bathroom Shaving

*I*t was now morning and he was in the bathroom shaving, shaving for the first time that day but not the last, no, never the last; the hairs kept coming, tiny hairs and black and there was nothing for it, nothing for it at all but shaving, razor bright-edged clean on skin and cutting through the hairs and the soap and the dead dried cells of epidermis in that clean well-lighted place. There were the hairs and he was shaving because a man shaves. Main thing a man did. Made him into a man. No bloody hairs.

She came in then, rich and tall and American in that way they have, her face a picture of a face, an American face, and she leaned into Gibbs Adams in that way she had of leaning, and he looked away from her American face in the mirror and down at the sink where she had just dropped the matchbook, the matchbook from Harry's Bar & American Grill.

"There wasn't going to be any of that," he said. "You promised there wouldn't be."

"Well, there is now," she said.

It's too damned awful, he thought, but there was nothing

for it, nothing at all but to shave and to take this woman with her American face to Harry's. And eat. They had eaten before. And the wine. Now, the wine. Well, the wine. Yes, the wine. Hm, the wine.

He looked at her bored American face in the mirror and knew they would eat, and there would be the wine, but there would never be the time in Venice, no, not that time again and no other. It was too late for that.

"What time is it?"

"5:05, Gibbs," she said, a good time, a big time, and he turned again to the mirror, to his American face in the mirror, his strong thin American face in the mirror with soap now drying on his skin, and the razor moving, scraping; and he could feel his hairiness now, the follicles open, ready, and he knew she knew them too, knew his hairiness and his thin American shame; and he saw his hand trembling in the glass and he felt the white-hot, blinding flash of metal, and that was all he ever felt.

He had cut himself about two inches up and a little to one side of the base of his chin.

He was bleeding now, the good, rich thin American blood red on his chin, on the razor, cold, gleaming, dripping on the matchbook, the Harry's Bar & American Grill matchbook, and he was afraid.

She turned, lifting her thin American lip over those thin white perfect American teeth in that thin American sneer. "It's only a nick, Adams," she said.

—Gordon Carlson

The Question Hung in the Air

► ► ► ► ► *T*he question hung in the air, stale and biting like the tang of cordite after an artillery barrage.

"Why do you do it the way you do?"

Always they must ask, no matter how many times they had heard the answer he had given others.

"The *Kansas City Star* style book," he said. He remembered the face of the city editor who had given it to him, a face pockmarked and riven by wrinkles born of too much whiskey and time.

She raised her heart-stopping eyebrows, still innocent of understanding.

" 'Keep it short,' the style book said."

She lit a cigarette, inhaled, her small and perfect breasts rising against the sheets, and blew a cat-gray jet of smoke toward the ceiling.

"Well," she said. "You certainly took that advice to heart."

He knew what they must do on this day. It was in a month with no *R*.

"Come," he said. "It is the day of the running of the oysters."

Her nose wrinkled as she came up from sleep, blinking her eyes, unconscious of the beauty that stirred him so. She reminded him of a rabbit he had killed, and he loved her nearly as much as the rabbit.

"It is three o'clock in the morning, Robert."

"We must arrive in time to pick scallions and drink a case or two of Margaux, then set up our post before the best terrain is taken."

"And then?"

"And then we will celebrate at Harry's Bar. Nicely."

They drove through the mist. It was a gray shroud, like those that hung over the Po that winter. He had made onion sandwiches and stuffed them into his pack with an apple each and a wedge of Fontina. She slept against his side. She was warm. He shifted gears as if he were squeezing a trigger. She could be flushed as easily as a young ring-necked pheasant on the first day of the season. He wanted to keep her with him always, or at least until Tuesday.

When she awakened, he explained about the running of the oysters. It was not a sport for young men. They are too impatient. They want to taunt the fry while they are still in their beds.

"I didn't know oysters could move, much less run."

He smiled his sad wise smile and stroked his beard. "Ah yes, they move. Before they set their beds where they will live. And die."

"And when they do move? What then?"

"That is the finest time, the time for cunning and courage," he said. He did not want to have to tell her about what would happen later, when the watermen came in sculling quickly through the beds, hungry eyes darting here and there for a glimpse of the fat juicy young flesh they lived for. Most of all, he did not want to tell her about the tongs.

—Lee Ewing

THE OLD MAN AND THE SEAL

*H*e was an old man who fished alone when he fished by himself. For 358 days now he had been fishless. Maybe if I used bait, he thought. And a hook. The last fish he caught was still in his pants pocket, forgotten.

"Qué stencho," the old man said. "No wonder I fish alone. But bad smell does not matter to a man, though this smell is very bad."

To the old man, the world had only two smells, the smell of the fish and the smell of the sea.

And the smell of no fish. Three smells.

He remembered the boy, who cooked *guazzetto* at Harry's Bar in Havana. The boy cared for the old man the way a woman would, though he was only a *boymano*, which is what people say in Spanish when someone is no longer a boy but not yet a man. He squeezed the shiny red ball the boy had given him.

"I am an old *bagowindo*," he reminded himself, "and I talk to myself. But maybe the great DiMaggio talks to himself too." The old man wondered if the great DiMaggio's conversations were as pointless as his own.

Then he saw the Big Fish.

Fish, you are my brother, the old man thought. At least you have the same moustache. He watched it swim in little loops, barking playfully. It jumped through the air, its black fur shining like the coat of a seal.

In fact, it was a seal.

"Now I know why the boy made me bring the ball," the old man said, tossing it overboard. "Fish, this is for you." While the seal was distracted, the old man slipped a rusty handcuff around its flipper.

"Fish, now we are truly linked." He laughed and wheezed and coughed.

They stayed handcuffed for a week. Then the seal began to tease the old man. It bounced the shiny red ball off the old man's old fisherman's nose, dry and callused from centuries of fishing.

"A man can be destroyed but not defeated," the old man said to the seal. Yes, that was the point of the story. "Or was it the other way around? The boy told me, but I forgot. *Qué dolto.*"

While the old man was talking, the seal climbed aboard and tossed him into the sea. It slipped out of the handcuffs and threw them to the old man.

"Great weight does not matter to a man," the old man gurgled, "but I wish these cuffs were made of aluminum."

"Sayonara," said the seal, which is what people say in Spanish when they mean "good-bye." Then it sailed back to Harry's Bar, got tight, and became best friends with the boy.

—*Mark Silber*

In the Late Summer of That Year
the Dressers and the Drapers

▶ ▶ ▶ ▶ ▶ *I*n the late summer of that year the dressers and the drapers and the changers in the wide trousers moved into the windows along the Via Tornabuoni. They wore long jackets, and sometimes short ones, and when they walked the jackets were wetted and then stained by the summer rain. They had come along this road before, in the spring, when things were going well. But now it was the end of summer, and the small buckles of *pastasciutta* that Vittorio made were gone, and the red taffeta chaps, and the panther-ear collars were gone, too. Now there were the terracotta socks that were very small, and the travertine belts that caught the light very finely, and the jade hats that were also very small and very fine.

We were walking, and then we crossed in front of the Strozzi and stopped in front of Stracci's. We watched the changers in the window, and then we watched ourselves watching the changers in Stracci's window. It had begun to rain again.

"It's no good," I said to Ashtry. "It's no good at all."

"Don't let's talk about it, darling," she said. "Don't let's talk about it at all." She was looking at the onyx boots.

"When you want the buckles, you can't have them," I said. "You never can."

"Buckles," she said. "But don't you see, darling? It's so terribly funny and brave. Now take a chap to Harry's Bar, where Adolfo's so good to us, and let's buckle one on."

We passed Santa Trinità and turned along the river. The street was lined with dead leaves, and they were the color of buckles and chaps.

"We're fine chaps, too, darling," I said. "Lovely, fine chaps. We're lovely, fine chaps without buckles, that's all."

The water in the river was low and brown and high and clear, and where it washed across the pebbles it made a sound like velvet on buckles.

"Do let's change the subject, darling," Ashtry said. "We're a pair of splendid chaps, and we've the small purses of plasticene, and the lovely caps of ivory, and the silk spats which are very small and white. Don't let's be unhappy, darling."

"No," I said. "Those were fine and lovely things, too. Now I'm happy."

But the size was wrong, or the color, or the strap was too long. Something was always wrong. We passed the bridge and I heard the water moving against its base. It was a good sound of hard, clean water and the water was buckling and unbuckling.

—*Brian Neilson*

She Is Truly One
of Magnificent Spirit

▶ ▶ ▶ ▶ ▶ *S*he is truly one of magnificent spirit, thought Ricardo, as the American woman called Louise broke a bottle of Campari over his head. She had short blond hair and was a bitch.

It had not always been so. Once she had long red hair and was a bitch. She drank Galestro from mason jars. It had been good then when they made love sweating and sweatingly on the pool table at Harry's Bar & American Grill and the balls had gone everywhere.

"Did you make the table move?" the bartender asked.

"Yes," Ricardo replied.

"Then you must move it back where it came from. There are others who want to make love."

The bartender placed the bowl back on the pig knuckles that glistened green and putrescent in the light from the single bulb hanging from the ceiling that cracked with age that came from neglect and a shortage of nonunion plasterers.

They left Venice that fall as the first winds lifted the feathers of the pigeons, then blew them into the canals, the little corpses riding the currents merrily around the pilings of the quay like drab bobbers in a cool Michigan trout stream.

There had been cockfights in Key West and pastrami sandwiches on the Borscht Circuit and the winter blizzards in Wyoming made it nearly impossible to find pheasant in the drifts. It had been good.

Now it was Paris and spring and Ricardo, looking at the water-stained glasses in back of the bar, knew it was a time of rebirth for him. It was time to leave.

"Good-bye," he said to the American woman Louise. "You have been my life. Truly, life has been a bitch."

—*Dave Eskes*

THE GRUNION STILL RAN
IN SANTA MONICA

▶ ▶ ▶ ▶ ▶ *T*he grunion still ran in Santa Monica, but we did not go there anymore. Before the English came and the rich Americans who talked too loud, it was good. The grunion came up on the beach and loved and died and no one made jokes about it. The true grunion *aficionados* stood on the wet side of the high tide line and drank the local beer and watched the grunion make love. Then the rich tourists came to sit on the dry side and drink the imported wine from San Francisco and laugh at the wrong time.

There are very few places left where men understand the running of the grunion. There is Harry's Bar & American Grill on the Avenue of the Stars which is a clean well-lighted place. That is the only rule at Harry's Bar: to say it is well-lighted and not to say it is well-lit. The Avenue of the Stars is well-lit, but you speak of the running of grunion in a place that is well-lighted. The English do not understand this, either.

There is a mountain between Santa Monica and the Avenue of the Stars. The old ones say that a grunion once climbed it, far above the high-tide line and died there, and when the smog lifts in the winter you can see it shining in the chaparral. No one knows why the grunion came so far from the ocean to a place where there is nothing to eat and no one to love. The old ones say it was going home to God. The young ones laugh and say it was going to Harry's to meet a woman.

I see nothing humorous in the death of a grunion. Some of them were very brave and some were very gentle on the sand at the time of the full moon when the earth moved and some were only foolish but the mountains of Santa Monica are impartial and kill all the ones that try to climb higher than Route 1. The others die on the beach. The tourists destroy them on the beach but the grunion are not defeated, only the mountain can defeat them. The grunion at the top was not even defeated. It was going somewhere and it only ran out of time, the least thing we have of.

—*M. R. Montgomery*

A CLEAN WELL-SIGHTED ACE

▶ ▶ ▶ ▶ ▶ *N*icholas Adams sat in the tall, green chair above the grass with the white lines and watched the two men dressed in white hit the ball over the net. Sometimes the ball hit the net and the ballboy ran across the green grass and picked the ball up and threw it to another ballboy. The men were practicing. They should play now, Nick thought.

"Play," Nick said.

The Swede stood at the line called the baseline and served the ball. Nick noticed that the ball was white and round and hung in the air a second before he hit it. The left-handed American hit it back. The Swede remained at the baseline through the whole point. On the grass it is not good for standing at the baseline. The game is fast and the serve and volley is the weapon for winning.

Soon the left-handed American ran to the net and the Swede hit the ball where he could not reach it.

"Fifteen–love," Nick said. Nick remembered the summer of '15 when he had played in Italy against the great Tilden. "Do not think about the double fault," the Old Man in the Stands had told him. The umpire warned the Old Man in the Stands about coaching. Nick double-faulted at match point. Later he sat with Tilden at Harry's Bar and drank Chianti. While he was remembering he missed the next point.

"Thirty–love," he said.

"What?" said the left-handed American.

"Thirty–love."

"The ball was out."

"The ball was good."

"That ball was out, you incompetent *obscenity*."

Nick did not say anything. He was embarrassed by the words "love," "ball," "out," and the expression "incompetent *obscenity*."

When play began again, the Swede served the ball and it hit a pebble and bounced away from the left-handed American.

"Forty–love," Nick said.

"That's not fair," the left-handed American said.

Nick heard the fear in his voice. What was it he feared? It was a nothing that he knew too well. It was all a nothing and man was a nothing and the American's score was a nothing which in tennis is love. When you have love, you have nothing, Nick thought. When you finished a match with nothing, you received no money. Except endorsements. There are always endorsements, Nick thought.

The Swede served very hard. The ball was a white flash. It reminded Nick of the soft puffs from the Austrian guns in the woods on the ridge near Milan. The ball hit the line. The linesman held both hands together, palms down. It was a clean well-sighted ace.

The left-handed American began to cry. "I am utterly unable to resign myself," he said and choked. He threw his racket into the stands. "I was sure the ball was going out. How could it have been good?"

"The earth moved," Nick said.

—Jay Jennings

The Last Good Martini

▶ ▶ ▶ ▶ ▶ *N*ick sat against the wall at Harry's drinking his dry martini with courage and with grace. The way a dry martini at Harry's should be drunk. In the mirror that is placed behind bars so a man can tell when he is drinking too much he saw her pull open the door and enter and she was there. He had not seen Frances Barnes since the war. She was blond and had tawny skin and a lean unblighted face. Nick thought she was very beautiful.

"Hello, Nicholas Adams," she said.

"Hello, Barnes," Nick said. "Do you want a dry martini? You used to drink them beautifully. Waiter, *due martini*, with garlic olives, not the big ones."

The waiter brought the martinis and they touched edges.

"Here's to the short happy life, Frances," Nick said.

"Say, Nick, that was grand. I was going to say chin-chin."

"Thank you for not saying chin-chin, nor bottoms up."

"You're welcome."

"Do you want to order dinner?" said Nick. "They still serve the big two-parted liver."

"Yes, thank you. That will be splendid," Frances said.

Ettore, with his emaciated face, came and took their orders and served them quickly and efficiently.

"What are you doing now, Nick? Still bowling?"

"Bowling well and writing well and other things are the only two important things in life," Nick said.

"I never understood why you really like to do this, this silliness of bowling."

Frances was beautiful but she was still dumb as hell, thought Nick. "The way to bowl," he said, "is for as long as you live against as long as a pin is standing in the lane. Do you remember George Tell?"

"Yes," said Frances. "He was a swell bowler. For Whom does Tell bowl now?"

"He bowls for my old man," Nick said. "He bowls straight and he bowls true but he still cannot hit a four-ten split with a handful of birdshot."

Frances laughed her good true laugh because of what she knew it did to him. He wanted to kiss her hard and well but he did not kiss her.

"And what have you been doing?" he asked.

"Still digging up stones and bones," she said. "I was looking for an alpine idol when I found this."

Frances took from her great huge bag a square stone covered with elaborate carvings. "What do you think?"

Nick looked across the liver and into the frieze and then remembered why his marriage to Frances Barnes had failed. Living with her had been like reading Sinclair Lewis before breakfast.

Frances finished her meal and rose to leave. "I don't suppose I will see you again," she said. It was a simple inquiry but Nick knew it meant the end of something. Nick said farewell to Barnes without regret as she turned and walked the other way from him.

"Ettore," he said, "put this nonsense on my bill."

—Daniel Hardy

Chapter 7

▶ ▶ ▶ ▶ ▶ *I*t was the summer of the middle of the war, but then we did not think it was the middle of the war because we thought it was near the end. It rained often and when it rained it rattled on the café awnings so we could not hear the Austrians tuning up in the mountains. After the rain there would be puddles in the awnings. When the rain stopped it would be hot and we would take walks around the piazza. I would make Isadora walk on the outside and when we came to an awning I would push up on the swollen part that was the puddle and the water would be dumped on her like the winter rains in Capri.

She was wet. The wool she wore was wet and in the hot afternoon it began to smell and there was the vapor burning off her sweater and we would walk together with her vaporizing in the sunlight. And when the wool was dry I would try to push her in front of bicycles. Once she turned and smiled at the old man on the corner who begged for Confederate postage stamps and I pushed her.

Later there were the crutches. There were the long crutches that she used for many weeks in the fall. There were no more walks. The war was closer now and we could hear the Austrian violins in the mountains. I knew they had a fresh battalion of timpani because Marcello had told me that the percussion section had been slaughtered in the spring by the mounted woodwinds we had seen riding through the piazza the day before the heat.

When Isadora could not take walks we went to Harry's Bar where it was cool and Marcello would try to kick her crutches away. But it did not matter because Isadora leaned on the bar and was steady and drank cool Swiss wines that were neutral. I sipped the pale yellow liquid with ice and it was cool and sour and it was grapefruit juice. Marcello had given me grapefruit juice and I had asked for Pernod.

"I *obscenity* in your cash register, Marcello," I said.

"It has been a wonderful summer," Isadora said.

"We have so little time and the war has been so slow and flat," I said. "But it has been fine to come here."

"It is sad for me. You have not paid me," Marcello said.

Three wounded piccolos entered and sat in the corner and I could tell that the percussion had gotten worse.

"Now, my love, we will leave and go back to my rooms and not be sad anymore," I said.

"It will be hard for me because although I love you I do not trust you."

I looked at her and saw her black eyes and cheeks smooth and red and shiny like the porcelain plates at the Hotel Des Cons. We went out to the sidewalk and I kissed her.

"There must be something greater for us, my love," she said.

I pushed her into a waiter who dropped his tray on top of the beggar. The beggar bent down to pick up his stamps in the puddle. I heard the sound of the Italian bassoons counterattacking in the third movement around the mountain.

You son of a bitch. I walked back to my hotel in the rain.

—*Robert B. Day*

A LEAN WELL-TIGHTED SPACE

▶ ▶ ▶ ▶ ▶ *I*t was early and those in the exercise room were still in the aerobic dance class except for a man older than the others who sat at the Nautilus machine for bulking up the pecs. On the wall was a poster of the great Stallone. The great Stallone's skin glistened with oil and his pecs bulged like the backs of boxer's gloves and his abs rippled like two croissants pushed together. The man was sweating but his skin did not glisten and his pecs did not bulge. He sat breathing hard for several seconds and then got up and wiped his face with a towel and walked to the machine for making the abs ripple. He walked holding his stomach in and tried to look at the aerobic dancers without turning toward them.

An attendant across the room spoke to another attendant who was adjusting the sound system.

"We ought to stop him from coming here."

"He's all right."

"It is a thing of concern to the girls. They come here to meet young men. They do not like to look at an old man. They do not like an old man looking at them."

"He's not so old."

"He must be forty-five at least."

"A man of forty-five may still like to look at girls."

"Let him go to the 'Y.'"

The second attendant shrugged. He finished with the sound system and began to check the bulbs in the panel of colored lights. It is not the same, he thought. Here the girls are lean and wear tights cut high to show the body on both sides of the groin. The girls at the "Y" have thick bodies and wear baggy sweat pants and are not good to look at like the girls one sees here at Harry's Bar & American Grill. A man should be able to choose his own space. It is important that the girls be lean and well-tighted.

The man finished with the last machine and picked up his towel and walked toward the showers. He walked like a man of forty-five but with dignity. He passed a group of girls wearing tights cut very high. He looked at the girls. The girls did not look at the old man.

It is all body, the second attendant thought to himself. Body *y pues* body. Our body who are in body. Body be thy name. Hail body full of body, body is with thee. *Pues* body. *Pobre viejo.* There must be many like that.

—*Fred D. Baldwin*

THE MARKET ALSO RISES

▶ ▶ ▶ ▶ ▶ *T*hat fall we lived in a brownstone in Manhattan and our love was stronger even than the Great Bull market which was our life and our joy. Although I spent many hours at the Street, we drove our BMW in the countryside on the weekends, and saw many shows and ate at fine restaurants and lived a life we hoped would never end.

"They say the Great Bull may reach 5,000 before it falls," she said, pouring another glass of Rioja. "May the Great Bull rise forever," I said, "and may we always work close to the Bull and never lose our quickness and nerve." But I knew it was a lie, for the world someday would break even the Great Bull, and if it could not break it then it would kill it, and perhaps it would kill us too but there would be no special hurry.

The day of the meltdown dawned bright and fair, but as it passed and the Great Bull lay in its blood in the sand, and everyone said "Oh muck," and not *"Olé,"* I knew it was mucked for good and higher than a kite. Oh, muck Wall Street and muck this whole treacherous muckfaced mucking market, and every mucking trader in it, insider and outsider, and to hell forever, I thought. Muck them to hell together, the SEC and the raiders and programmed trading, and all of them.

At the end it wasn't any good and I went out and left the Street that evening and walked back to our apartment in the rain. When I returned, she knew not of the greatness of our loss. "For whom did the closing bell toll?" she asked.

"You know not of this of the market?" I said. "I know," I said. "But if we lose here, then we lose everywhere. The market is a fine place and worth the trading for, and I hate very much to leave it."

"But what will become of us?" she asked. I could not answer. "We could go to Florence," she said.

Life, I thought, is never a done deal. But perhaps in Florence there would be a separate piece of action. "Yes," I said, my spirit rising, "we will go to Florence. For the pasta futures."

"Yes," she said, "and for the winter sports."

"And for Harry's. For Harry's and for the pasta and the *calamaretti fritti*."

The next day, we sold the Bimmer and our Rolexes, our Mont Blancs, and even the espresso maker. "We won't need it in Florence," she said. "Yes," I said, "isn't it pretty to think so?"

—*Mark A. Sherouse*

THERE ARE NO TROUT
IN THE MARTINIS

*H*e was an old man and he had not had a martini in eighty-four days. He could have had many martinis in other bars, but it would not have been the same. In those bars you drank beer or drinks with little umbrellas goring fruit. You did not drink the martini.

Now he was in the right bar and the martini was before him and it was clear and chilled and it reminded him of the cold streams in Spain where he would fish for trout. He could see the trout in the chilly water and how they would come to the bait. But that was now over. He was old and the fishing was over.

"There are no trout in these martinis," he said to the young couple at the table next to him. He did not know them, but he knew they were young and would not understand what it was like to have fished and then not be able to fish. The couple looked at their martinis and then at him.

He looked at the woman. Women reminded him of boats. Some women were like expensive yachts or cruise ships. Others, beautiful sailboats with full white sails. There were the wrecks, too, sunken and covered with barnacles and seaweed and wormy. The woman at the table next to him reminded him of a speedboat.

But the women were gone now. The man and woman at the table would not understand about the women being gone, but he said to the couple, "There is not a woman sitting in the chair there." The couple looked at the empty chair, then at the old man and then at each other.

The old man thought about the woman poet in Paris who had taught him to write the true sentence. He had sent her a rose as a gift and she had sent him four thank-you notes. She was a mystery vessel in the fog. Why the four notes?

But he thought again about fish. The brave fish and the unbrave fish. A goldfish was not a brave fish and he said to Speedboat, "A goldfish is not a brave fish. And there aren't even any goldfish in my martini."

The couple finished their martinis in the wrong fashion, the old man thought. You did not drink the martini in Harry's Bar as they did. You drank such a martini slowly. Otherwise it was the same as entering the bull ring and killing the bull with a tommy gun. He started to tell the couple about how wrong it was to use a tommy gun in the bull ring, but after drinking their martinis in the wrong fashion, they left and he was now alone with his memories and the martini in this clean well-lighted place.

—*Robert H. Robinson*

A Farewell to Arms
(and Legs and Feet and Neck . . .)

A light rain fell. A light rain that was gray. A light, gray, wet rain. I saw her there—or so I thought—standing by the bar. A good bar. A bar with an American grill. Harry's Bar & American Grill. I ate slowly of my dessert, watching her fade in and out. She came over to me while still opaque. "Sit down," I said before she could speak. "Thank you," she said sadly as she sat. There was something in her voice. Something I could not pin down. "My name is Katherine."

"Would you like to share my cake?" I asked as I pushed the plate toward her.

"No, I would prefer a separate piece," she answered. As if that told me everything. As if that could stop her pain. As if I cared. We ordered.

Outside the rain continued to fall. She watched it come. Often she frowned, fading out at the edges. I did not understand her. Mostly, I could not see her. It was not that Katherine was shallow. She was, rather, poorly defined. So poorly defined that she often disappeared. I tried to speak with her.

"Does the rain disturb you?" I asked.

"No, but sometimes I think I see . . ." her voice trailed off as her mouth disappeared.

And then I knew. She must see Death there. Dripping, wet Death. What else would one see in the rain?

She continued as she reappeared, ". . . little rainbows. I see little rainbows in the rain." Her thoughts then, like her character, were not complex. We continued to eat.

Suddenly she pleaded with me, "I do not like to get wet!"

"We are inside." I was confused. "You will not get wet."

She laughed, a funny laugh. A laugh to make you cry. Unless you were a man. Then she became fuzzy again.

I looked down. She made me sad. I did not know how to please her. I did not think I should have to. I reached for her hand but it was gone. So were her arms. And in her eyes was a look that said "Farewell." Whether it was to me or to her arms I will never know. Soon only her mouth remained. A mouth that was smiling. A sad, odd smile. A smile that echoed the final word, "Farewell."

I walked out into the Cheshire night, as men do, into the darkness, into the rain, into a cab and went home.

—*Maryann Martone*

OUT OF THE POOL
AND INTO THE SUNLIGHT

▶ ▶ ▶ ▶ ▶ *E*rnest looked across the pool. Two little ones flashed brightly in front of him. At the rear the big ones were dim shadows. They were feeding slowly. Ernest looked into the blankness. His wound hurt. He flicked his wrists. The green line cast out. On the line were words like "courage," "honor," "despair," "Yoknapatawpha" and "Faulkner." They were the big words. They were the bad words. They were obscene.

Ernest said, "I *obscenity* in the milk of these mothers." He flicked his wrists. The big bad words disappeared. Only the blankness was there. It was like the swamp.

He flicked his wrists again. The green line cast out. On the line were new words. They were words like "bitch" and "bull" and "pasta" and "vino" and "rose" and "rose" and "rose" and "Stein." They were the little words. They were the good words. They made his wound hurt less.

Ernest looked to the rear of the pool. The big ones were still feeding slowly. They were eating what Plato had brought from The Cave. It was garbage. Ernest felt bad. He was hungry. That was no good. The food at Harry's

Bar & American Grill was good. It made his wound hurt less.

In the front of the pool the two little ones flashed brightly. They were good like the little words. They were the keepers. "Maria, Marlene," Ernest said. "Daughters, today we lunch at Harry's."

"*Sí,* Ernesto." *"Ja, Vater,"* they said. "We shall eat and drink well. We shall not behave badly. We shall behave well like the good little words."

Ernest turned off his word processor. The green line was gone. The screen was blank like the swamp. The big bad words were deleted. The big dim secretaries were like the big bad words. They were slow and lazy. They were no good. They would be fired late afternoon.

Ernest caught the two bright little secretaries. They went out of the typing pool and into the sunlight. "Your probation is over," he said. "You will get raises next week."

Ernest and Maria and Marlene got into the Bugatti Royale and made for Harry's. The good little words were stored in files on diskette. Ernest would write them into stories after lunch. The stories would be good and strong like the drinks at Harry's.

They made his wound hurt less.

—*Richard D. Lynde*

THE MAN LAY ON THE ROOF
OF THE CONDOMINIUM

▶ ▶ ▶ ▶ ▶ *T*he man lay on the roof of the condominium building and stared down at the dentist's office. "I do not remember this medical building," he said. "The old taco stand was below, near to the freeway."

"It was built since you were here, *Inglés*. It is where the men go for the bridges and the crowns."

He remembered the words that Golz had told him. "Anyone can make a bridge, but to do just that is a failure. But to make the bridge at a stated time in a manner for which the *gente* will pay you—that is how it should be done."

The old woman turned to him. "*Inglés,* they say that the *doctor* and his receptionist can smell the smell of decay. Dost thou know what that means, *señor? Comprendes?*"

"I have never smelled such an odor," answered Robert.

The gypsy woman looked at him mockingly. "All right, *Inglés.* To imagine such a smell, thou must first go to the place where the subway stops at exactly 5:45 P.M. on a hot afternoon in July. Thou must go into the crowd of laborers who stand side by side in the car at Sixty-Eighth Street and inhale thy breath deeply. That is the first part of the smell. Dost thou want to hear more?" asked the gypsy woman.

"Surely," he said. "You are my Pilar of strength."

"Hast thou been in a locker room where there is no deodorant, *señor*? When the men who play the *fútbol* have not yet showered? Plunge thy nostrils into it and thou will learn the second part of the scent."

The general came out to the roof. "It is time, *Inglés,* time to go and get the bridge. Do not be afraid. *Tengo uno también,*" he said. "I have one too."

Later that day, Robert awoke. He had spat in the sink like the other men. He had the bridge and it was all right. *"Está bien,"* he had told the receptionist. "Have a nice day," she had replied. Perhaps it was a superstition.

He went to Harry's Bar to celebrate. "I drink against dentists who are incorporated," he thought. "Against stereo headphones, old magazines, pastel uniforms, Muzak, 'A tooth that's flossed is seldom lost,' and 'It is customary to pay for professional services when they are rendered.'"

Soon the gypsy woman would join him and they would together make a toast *to* something—to the novocaine and the Blue Cross.

Meanwhile, he would read the old *National Geographic* and the *People* and drink the rum. The pain had already begun to subside.

—*Paula Van Gelder*

He Was Happy That
Nature Was Redundant

► ► ► ► ► *H*e was happy that nature was redundant when the bullet smashed into his left kidney.

It hurt, but not much.

Why doesn't it happen to the rich? he wondered.

The rich, he thought, are always talking about their kidneys. Especially the English rich.

The plane lost altitude fast. It slammed into the rocks. A steel rod rammed through a portion of his liver.

The French are not always talking about their livers, he thought.

It hurt but not much. He stood there rubbing ruefully at his kidney and liver.

The pilot revved the engine. Flames engulfed them.

"I don't know what to do," he said.

"God!" she said, "don't be stupid. Use your head."

He broke open a window with his head.

His head hurt but not so much.

He felt his knees and they were broken. Then he saw her unconscious. He carried her to one side. There was not much time to think of knees, anyway.

He set her down, then ran back to the burning plane and

got the bottle of absinthe and the canteen of martinis he'd got from Harry's Bar. His arms and face were hot and his beard flamed.

He stopped to drink the martinis from the canteen.

The martinis were not cold. They were very warm. It was unbearable.

He began to cry.

—Hannah Sampson

THE OLD MAN IN THE YARD

▶ ▶ ▶ ▶ ▶ "*Y*ou must come in now, Sánchez," the old man said. Sánchez did not move and he knew that he must not show his fear. He pulled harder on the chain, but the dog did not want to enter the warm *casa*.

"Dog, you are trying to kill me," he said aloud as he stood by the lilac bush and thought about the great Marlin Perkins. He knew the punishment of the chain was nothing for someone as proud as Sánchez. He was a strong dog, but not as intelligent as the one who walked him. He thought about the dog biscuit in his pocket, but he knew it was better to save it for an emergency. "That's foolish," he told himself. It was such a cold night and he worried he was no longer clear-headed. He had been out for eighty-four minutes and he knew he was strong enough to stay out longer, but the weather was turning worse. He wished he were drinking a warm cappuccino with Maria at Harry's Bar & American Grill. The dog looked at the back door and the old man thought, I will say three Hail Marys if the dog goes in by himself. He looked at his left hand and thought, Rest now, old man, and the next time you pull, he will come for sure.

Sánchez moved slowly toward the house. This is what I have waited for, he thought. The boy should be here now to help me. He loved the boy and wondered why he was never around when someone needed him. "You think too much, old man," he said to himself. He put his two hands together and pulled hard.

"I will bring you in, Sánchez. I will fight you until I die." His hands were sore and he worried he would have to pull hard again, but his arms and shoulders were still strong. He did not want the dog to see the cramp in his left hand. He must not know it is only one old man against him. He put his right hand over his left and entwined them in the leash. You went out too late, he thought, and pulled again on the chain. As Sánchez ran out the back gate into the darkness of the alley, he began to pity the strange dog.

"Full-sized dog that you were. I have ruined us both." He walked up the porch steps and lay down in bed. He was asleep when the boy came in in the morning. The sun was shining. The boy looked at the old man's hands and started to cry.

"The dog beat me, Pedro." He noticed how much nicer it was to talk to a boy instead of a dog.

"Rest, old man," the boy said. "I will bring you some coffee. Soon your luck will change." The boy went into the kitchen and cried again. When he returned, the old man was sleeping and dreaming about cats and litter boxes.

—Gloria Golec Merbitz

A Clean Well-Lighted Race

▶ ▶ ▶ ▶ ▶ *I*t was the hour of the *camarones*. Jimmy put a plate of the big ones out at seven, and we cracked the thin shells deliberately with our fingers and stacked the shells beside the plates for Jimmy to sweep behind the counter. The Riojo blanco was cool, even in the heat. We drank largely of its flavor of zinc, and I remembered another place where the wine was not so good but they make the *pez espada* with rosemary. Later, we would go there for the fish and to talk of how the wine was not so good as here. There are many hours in a day.

Earlier, there had been the running of the roaches in the Plaza de Cucarachas. Before, waiting under the strong sun, we had bet on the outcome. Tess had favored the big black they called El Cubano, but I could see from the flanks there was no juice in him. There is a way one knows these things, which one can learn. But some cannot learn. Once, but it was in another time, I sat with the old man all day watching in the light. He was an old man from the Basque country who drank too much but who could tell one about the lines. So, with his eyes, I could see the light move on the nervous one, the brown-with-lemon-spots some called Manchita. I said, "I will bet this small amount on Manchita," and Tess had laughed the full, rich laugh of her womanhood. It was good to be sitting there and to hear the laugh in the plaza with many friends.

While we sat cracking the *camarones*, I saw in the doorway the tall Greek with gold teeth they call Avgolemono, but not in his face. It is not good to say such things in a man's face. I remembered how, once, but in another time, he had stopped at my table in Harry's Bar & American Grill, and how we had spoken of things men speak of, of the Galliano with a twist, of the lemon sole one brought to the table with the fire yet on it. We spoke of how the taste of earth and that of the sea came from them and of the yellow in Giotto and Mantegna and the things men speak of. But there was no luck for me in this Greek, I knew. I did not like this second meeting, though it is not good to say so in a man's face.

Seeing us, he came over.

So there was no way. I did what a man must.

"Tess," I said, "this is Mr. Didaktyliaios."

After the silence had spoken for him, he spoke to her.

"You must call me Dak, my dear; shall I call you Contessa?"

Then, there was her laugh, again, a great white comber breaking in slow motion on Baltic stone, and I had the first fear.

She said, "Call me Tess, short for Tessitura . . . Dak."

I remembered the Galliano with a twist before the lemon sole at Harry's Bar & American Grill in Florence. But today had been the running of the roaches in a border town the

Guardia Civil do not like to visit. There had been the small amount I had placed on the brown-with-lemon-spots. There had been the large amount she had placed. El Cubano with the male bigness, which is why she liked him. Manchita had not the bigness but there was this thing in the light, this thing the Basque had made my eyes to see. Less can be good, but it is not so for a woman, a woman with much need. That is how it was with Tess.

So there was no way. The next day, she went with Avgolemono. At her going, I said nothing. We had said all that was good. To break clean is the way of the boxing ring; it is the way a man and a woman learn, if they are wise, and if it has been good.

Now, I can stand no yellow. In the street, I look away from the tourists with their yellow shirts, the boxes of Kodak film. I do not eat the eggs, for their yolks disgust me. And the lemon sole, the Galliano with a twist, I leave to the ones who come to Harry's Bar & American Grill to hear the things I say, who smile their hard young smiles. They do not smile in my face, for it is not good to smile in my face, yet I know.

A day has many hours. How could a man not know?

—*Stuart J. Silverman*

A FAREWELL TO LUNCH

▶ ▶ ▶ ▶ ▶ *H*e was an old restaurant reviewer who ate alone at a corner table and always gave a different name when he called for reservations. For twenty nights now he had eaten nothing that deserved more stars than the nachos of 7-Eleven, and he wondered when his luck would change.

At first he had not wanted to write about restaurants. He had told the editor that it was not a thing that a man could get down on paper. That was why the high-priced fakes jabbed and feinted with words like "zesty" and "tangy" and "succulent." Only after many nights of trying the food and thinking could you know. And when you knew, just the smallest taste of a marinara sauce with its fine green flecks of basil would tell you whether the chef was a fool or a man to be admired. No *crítico* could give you that.

But he had eaten and had written and had lasted. He met the grilled mahi mahi in its beurre blanc sauce and, much later, he took on the charbroiled swordfish at Santiago's on the Square. One day at a new sushi bar the hellish green mustard had fought his guts like a manta ray. Still he had made his deadline and the copy was on the editor's desk before he could hold his lunch no more. When he was strong again and in a fine mood, he took the girl to La Testosteroni for lunch.

The bad luck was draped around his neck like the dead bird in old Sam T. Kohlrabi's poem. The salmon *a la stimpirata* was drier than a temperance meeting in Utah and the buttered *camarones* had no *cojones*. The woman knew what had happened and did not look at him. Instead she looked out the window at the rain.

"It was not so bad," she said after a while.

"No," he said. She was not like the ones who smell a man's hurt like the sharks smell blood in the sea.

"The lettuce. The arugula. It could have had more snap."

"Yes," he said.

"What is for dessert?" He could not look at the chalkboard for its daily specials.

"They have the fine white chocolate cheesecake that brought you the moments of joy in Milan. Remember?"

He said nothing. Milan had been a long time ago, before the war.

She looked at him. "Let's go to Harry's for a drink. We always laugh at Harry's."

"No. I must write the review."

When she left he sat alone at the table and slowly chewed a few bites of her cheesecake. It made him think of Milan so he ordered a separate piece. *Nada. Nada.* Nothing had been zesty or succulent and he did not feel like people-watching.

"*Nada. Nada,*" he said.

"Nada is off tonight, sir," the waiter said. "She only works weekends now."

The thing to do was to leave. After a while he paid the check and walked back to the newspaper in the rain.

—Chris Tucker

REST IN THE AFTERNOON

▶ ▶ ▶ ▶ ▶ *T*he old man sat at the bar, stalking his drink. The drink was at the edge of the bar, nearly resting on the old man's chest. He could smell its breath. The old man could not get up. Not now. Not without spilling everything.

The bar was called Harry's Bar and it was a good place for the drinking sport because the bartender understood what there was to know about hard, honest martinis and that made the writing not hurt as much as it could. The writing was a bitch. The old man confided this to his drink. It was a lioness bitch that waited for you in the deep grass of your own thoughts and dared you to wade into the grass. In the grass there was fear and confusion and if you approached it badly the lioness would destroy you. You had to enter the grass straight and clean, with sentences that were simple and declarative and they could never be pretty. If you did not write it this way then they would say that you were cheating. So you had to get rid of the flowery prepositional phrases and the big comfortable words and go in stripped naked except for the one weapon you were allowed to take in with you: the word *and.* You were allowed to use that to make a sentence longer if you wanted to and then it would look braver and more able to survive. You could, if you really wanted to, put in a lot of *and*s, they didn't count, and with luck the sentence never had to end, you could go on and on, and tell the story that a man had to tell and say what had to be said about birth and love and death and whoring and women and whiskey, and do that with grace or arrogance or cynicism or however you wanted to do it, and never worry about whether the parts of your story really made any sense or even whether they went together syntactically, because ultimately the middle of a long sentence is like the middle of an ocean, you will have lost sight of both the shore that is behind you and the one that is ahead of you but in the end it doesn't matter because *you are here* except finally you are talked out and you don't want to say any more, or you have no more time for it and it is not good in you, but you don't know how to stop anymore, to turn the writing off and let the damned sentence die the death it was meant to die.

That is why it is best to keep the sentences short, he thought. A really big sentence could get away from you and then you would have nothing to show for it. All that would be left of your writing would be the big stench of your effort. The beast that waits for you in the grass knows the stench well. That is why we will not write more for today. It is safer now to drink. Bartender. F—k the lioness bitch.

—Richard S. Simons

A Short, Happy Hike

▶ ▶ ▶ ▶ ▶ *He* was crossing Ducy Basin and the backpack was hard on his shoulders and he felt strong and good and without age. She was trying to meditate as she hiked, and when she walked into him he laughed, but his laughing was stopped by her sadness, which rent him like the quick horn of a flaring-nostrilled bull.

"Alone, my little squirrel?" he asked, thinking too of winter.

"I'm carrying Anaïs Nin," she said. "It's next to my granola."

He did not know Granola, though he had admired Pirandello. She had just spent a weekend with someone named Werner, apparently running a marathon, yet still seemed fragile and full of a woman's need. She turned back with him down the trail toward the Evolution Valley.

"I was rolfed last week," she said, pitifully. "Hard."

He felt for her then, though he didn't know what it was to be rolfed. He had been gone a long time. He assumed it was their new word for sexual coupling, and he was stirred. He looked at her legs. There were varicose veins, but they were good varicose veins. They reminded him of a map of the Spanish countryside he had carried in the war. It was all a long time ago.

"You will be all right, my little marmot," he said. "I will take you to Harry's."

She moved so close that her Sierra cup pressed against his Swiss Army knife. He didn't rearrange it, though he might have in another year, when things were different.

"It is singles?" she asked.

"For us," he said, "it's togethers."

—*John M. Wilson*

HILLS LIKE WHITE HEFFALUMPS

▶ ▶ ▶ ▶ ▶ *T*he hills across the valley of Pooh Corner were long and white. On one side there was no shade and no trees and a stuffed animal could fry in the heat in minutes. A small building stood between the valley and the green Hundred Acre Wood. A bear and the girl with him sat at a table in the shade, outside the building.

"What should we eat?" the girl asked.

"Honey," said the bear. It was hot and small beads of sweat dropped off the tip of his nose. He watched the water make a reasonable pool on the table. He looked up at the girl.

"It will be all right," she said. "Lots of people have done it."

"I don't know," said the bear. He thought about the war. He tried not to think, but it was always there in the darkness. He remembered the explosion and afterward the doctors putting the stuffing back inside him. He remembered the months in the Pet Hospital on Santa Monica Boulevard in Century City, and afterward the walks to Harry's Bar & Grill in the afternoon. He remembered the old waiter and the young waiter and how no one ever quite learned how to say the Lord's Prayer without all the *nada*s in it.

"Oh, pooh," swore the girl. "I can't bear it when you're like this."

The bear looked across at the hills in the distance. They looked like white heffalumps. He smiled to himself, remembering how clever things had been before the accident. Now his old friends were all gone. Everyone had become a therapist specializing in manic depression. Tigger had opened an aerobics studio in Beverly Hills. Kanga had finally gotten the divorce settlement and moved back to Australia. The bear realized he was thinking too much. He crossed his legs carefully and stared at the girl.

The waitress brought a jar of honey. The bear stuck his nose in it and began to eat.

"Don't get your head stuck in the jar," the girl said. "Like last time."

The bear looked down across the valley. Everyone's gloomy place had been subdivided and overbuilt with condos. He remembered hunting for woozle on crisp winter mornings when his breath would frost in the air and he would follow tracks in the snow and the world seemed so clear and true that it was like being in love all the time. He tried to remember what being in love was like but his accident had fixed that and the girl was talking again and he couldn't think.

"It's an awfully simple operation," she said. "And then everything would be like before."

The bear stood and looked down at the sleek unbroken line of fur that ran to his toes. "Yes," he said. "Isn't it pretty to think so?"

—*Chris McCarthy*

THE OLD MAN WROTE VERY WELL

► ► ► ► ► *T*he old man wrote very well. He knew he wrote very well because the old man had studied hard the penmanship and always stayed between the lines when he colored. He had been across the river and into the trees and within the house that Jack built.

He was a savvy old man and did not spit against the wind or lead with his right or put beans in his ears. He did not like to shoot things but did not feel it would be held against him by anyone, except perhaps a duck. And ducks did not sit on prize committees.

Mostly.

When the old man wrote well it was like the fine steaks at Harry's Bar & American Grill or the meatballs and spaghetti at Tony's on Sixty-Eighth Street, but sometimes he overwrote and it was like the corned beef at Hugo's by the cod factory, the corned beef and the cabbage and those little dessert tarts or fruit cups or whatever the hell they were, the ones with the wet cigar shreds on them. Then the old man did not smell like a rose unless the breeze was behind you, which was a good thing until the old man surprised you, and you quickly recalled an appointment in Alamo-gordo, New Mexico.

The old man wrote of the *corrida* and of the *bandarilleros* and the bull in the afternoon.

He wrote much about the bull.

The bull was everywhere.

—William Ruehlmann

HARRY'S BAR & AMERICAN GRILL
IS A CLEAN WELL-LIGHTED PLACE

▶ ▶ ▶ ▶ ▶ *H*arry's Bar & American Grill is a clean well-lighted place. You can buy a moveable feast there for under fifty grand when you're paying in lira. And with a crowd truly it feels like the capital of the world. Outside if the weather is nice, the sun also rises as it does each day across the green hills of Africa and above the snows of Kilimanjaro. Before today I'd never been to Harry's Bar & American Grill. I'd never been to the Garden of Eden either.

Inside I was deciding whether to have or to have not. I had bidden my farewell to arms and from out of the trees had crossed over the Arno to get to a table near one of the five columns that held Harry's up. In that clean favorable light of the world I had just walked into I was sure there would be no more death in the afternoon. And for me no more men without women.

It was raining when I came in. From my seat I imagined the old man now at sea, his boat grunting across a hard gray surface out where the big fish would be running. He would be trolling, and I pictured him standing at the bridge poring over the hard swells looking for the big fish to come as he would know they would right after the storm. He could be thinking about last night and about the drinking at Harry's. He could be thinking, too, how no man seemed to know who he was anymore. Or really care. Maybe, I thought, he could finally see how he had become a way you or I would never be, a winner who gives and who takes nothing.

Sitting in Harry's I recalled the old man's short happy life and the fishing we did in our time up in Michigan when he was a real battler before the killers came and chased him up the big two-hearted river and then cut out to sea. Well and with grace. After all the fishing we did among the rocks that were shiny and very smooth and like small islands in those streams.

Suddenly I stopped remembering. I could hear a bell tolling. For whom it tolled I couldn't tell. It could have been tolling for thee. Or for me. Right then I ordered a bottle of wine, a red dark wine that I wanted to be honest and good like wines I'd had in all the places I'd been in that served honest and good and truly dark wines. Wines that poured like torrents that sometimes came down in the spring. I waited in Harry's for the good dark wine to come still wondering about the old man out there riding the sea alone and waiting for the great fish to come.

—Chet Seymour

YOU KNOW HOW IT IS

▶ ▶ ▶ ▶ ▶ *Y*ou know how it is when the old drunk finds his place at the foot of the great seated Arsenale lion and the proprietor of the Bar Arsenale puts out the little metal tables with the Campari umbrellas and the young Italian sailors stand at the counter to have their morning cappuccino and to talk about the girls they had had last night, or about their mammas, because they are mostly from the country and not really Venetians, in spite of their im-maculate uniforms, white and very beautiful. That summer one of the sailors would always buy an espresso for the old drunk so he would not roar as he sat on the base of the great stone lion, his eyes sad and distant like the lion's as they both looked toward the Lido, past the tourist liner from Dubrovnik listing toward San Biagio.

"Let him roar and look sad in his own *sestiere*," said the first sailor. He pushed aside the bead curtain of the doorway and the beads, on which were printed a Campari bottle and a girl, faded but very lovely, rustled as the sailor reached out to crush his cigarette on the table where Will and I were finishing our first *prosecca*.

"No," said the second. "He is a clean old man despite

his drunkenness and perhaps he is someone's uncle. Besides, today I have brought something for him, something that will take his mind from his sorrow."

"Accidenti," the first sailor said. The second sailor took a small object from his pocket and gave it to the old drunk and I could see that it was a *joujou,* or yo-yo, the kind they were selling to the American tourists in the Piazzetta that summer, that when you pulled it apart and fitted two AA batteries into the clear plastic halves it would give a lovely orange light that would move my heart and I knew I would have to go every day to see the great Carpaccio *Miracolo* in the Accademia.

"Say, Rick," said Will. "What about this Lady Gritt business?" The old drunk was doing a very fine Buzzer with the yo-yo against his left shoe and the metal eyelets gave out lovely sparks like the fireworks they would be setting off very soon from the great barges in the Canale della Giudecca at the Festa del Redentore.

"I don't give a damn about that anymore." I signaled the waiter. *"Cameriere, due cappuccini, per piacere."* Although I was very fond of watching the old drunk in the Campo Arsenale, it was not like having cappuccino at Harry's Bar, where you enter from the Calle Vallaresso and you know everything will be wise and generous and fine, part of Venice surely but the best part of a world.

The drunk was leaning over the railing of the Ponte di Purgatorio and he roared as the Number One *vaporetto* approached and he let down the yo-yo in a lovely, trembling arc, and I remembered how the string, loosely tied around the axle would throb, soft but deadly, as you tossed it out for Around the World or Walking the Dog, and the low roar of the great African lion as you watched him from the blind, tightening the rough cotton string around the yo-yo's shaft for your one Bull's Eye shot, the only shot you knew he would let you have.

"You aren't sore I asked about the Lady Gritt?" said Will. He added "Lady" to her first name because he was not very bright even though I was very fond of him.

"Why the hell should I be?" We had had to walk for five days through the lovely Ardennes woods and the Germans crouching high in the tall great beech trees had filed the edges of their steel *Kletterkreisel,* or yo-yos, razor sharp and it wasn't until the fourth day that we knew you had to keep anything that protruded from you pulled in, and it probably wasn't until the sixth day that the wild boar rooting for truffles in the very lovely autumn woods had found it among the brass buttons and noses in the rotting leaves, and when Gritt left me at the Ponte di Rialto on the arm of the dark young gondolier Giacomo, straight and pure and unsmiling in his straw boater and striped jersey, and said, "You rather don't mind, do you, Rick darling, though it might have been rather lovely?" then there was nothing left for me to say but no, not at all; why the hell should I.

—*Lois Baker*

The Champ

The Only Good Spaniard

▶ ▶ ▶ ▶ ▶ *I*t was a hot day, the sun shining and the ground baking and the sweat on our backs.

"It is a hot day," said Rosalita, "and I have the thirst."

"It is not so hot," I said. "There is no need for the thirst."

"The thirst is large within me." Rosalita pointed a gun at my head.

"It is good," I said. "It is good you have the thirst."

I was in the pay of the *revolucionarios* and I fought for the Republic. I did not fight for the Republic because I loved the Republic. I fought for the Republic because there was good pay from the Republic for those who fought for the Republic, even if they did not love the Republic.

Rosalita did not approve of this.

Now Rosalita wore a black peasant's smock and gray, stiff trousers. A belt of cartridges went across her smock from the shoulder to the hip. Her hair was cut short, and the corners of her eyes crinkled when she smiled or when she cut the ears off an enemy of the Republic. She was damned good-looking, for one who had the thirst.

"I know where you can quench the thirst," I told Rosalita.

We stood up and Rosalita put her gun away and we started across the field. It was a hot day, the sun on our backs.

"Where are we going?" said Rosalita.

"Harry's," I said. "There you can quench the thirst."

"What is this Harry's?"

"Don't talk about it or you'll lose it."

After the field was the wood and the ridge of hills and the stream alongside the road and then the bluffs and the Atlantic Ocean and Europe. Harry's was not close to the Republic.

Inside Harry's Bar & American Grill was a bar and an American grill and many tables. We sat at one of the tables and a waiter came to our table. The waiter's name was Bill.

"How about a nice stuffed dog?" said Bill. "We can grill it on the grill."

"We are out of the Republic," I said.

Then we had a good meal: a roast chicken, new green beans, mashed potatoes, some apple pie, and fourteen bottles of Chablis. Rosalita no longer had the thirst. Rosalita slept under the table.

"Because you are of the Republic," said Bill, "there will be no bill." He tore up the bill.

"No bill?" I said.

"No bill," said Bill.

"You are noble," I said.

"No, I am Bill," said Bill. "But there will be no bill."

"Thank you," I said. I kicked Rosalita under the table.

"Huh?" said Rosalita.

"Let us go," I said.

I said good-bye and Rosalita said good-bye and Bill said good-bye. Now we would have the walk home and the swim across the Atlantic Ocean.

—Marcus Webb

Only More So

*I*t was a dark wet night. Gerty Stein would have called it a dark dark wet night night. But I'm not Gerty. I'm Nick.

I entered Harry's Bar. It was dark and wet. In my last story it was clean and well-lit. I never repeat myself.

I ordered a banana daiquiri. "Make it a double; I'm depressed," said Nick.

"A minute ago you were in first person," said the bartender.

He was right. Bartenders are always right. Particularly Spanish bartenders.

"Catch any big fish lately, *amigo?*" It was Lardo. Lardo fought bulls. His skin was the color of meatloaf. His hands were as supple as a steelworker's.

"No," I replied.

"I see," said Lardo.

Lardo saw. I did not. I punched him in the mouth. It was a good punch. A big punch. A punch as big and good as the haunches of a female elk in rutting season. Lardo fell. He fell well. All Spaniards fall well.

"Why did you do that, *amigo?*" he said.

"I don't know."

It was good I don't know. I sat down at the bar like any other man, only more so, and chugged my daiquiri.

"Oh hell," I muttered and threw the straw away.

Lardo got up from the floor.

"Amigo?" he said.

"Yes?" I replied.

"I am a man."

"Yes, Lardo, I know you are a man."

"Then you know what I must do."

"Yes, I know."

With that, he struck my unshaven writer's chin with his supple bullfighter's fist. As he did, I could hear a bell toll in the distance. My body hit the floor hard. I wondered who the bell was tolling for.

"Whom," said the bartender.

—Steven Spivak

IT HAD BEEN A GOOD WINTER

▶ ▶ ▶ ▶ ▶ *I*t had been a good winter. Hard and white and cold, yet fine in its coldness like the Irati where they fished in the summer when the air was warm but the river was cold and the trout that they had caught would lie gleaming like fine sculpted ice on the grass. This winter was cold and fine in that way.

When they were not enjoying the fine coldness of the winter they did other things. He sat in a cubicle and stared at a machine. He would write the software and design the system and dream of buying the small truck called Mazda.

She would sit in a cubicle and stare at a machine, but this was in another part of the city. It was along the rue de Kazootie where the good frozen yogurt shops are, and the expensive haircuts. Sometimes she would feel the small kicking and the hard elbowing inside and then she would know that the baby was awake. That was always good, even when it brought the Heartburn, or the Big Queasy.

"*Menos* Maalox," she would say, and it would be good again.

The winter still was good and cold and fine even when she missed seeing the ice, the gleaming thin ice which shone like the nose of the bartender at Harry's. The ice was small, but it was bad. It was enough.

"Obscenity, obscenity," she said as her ankle snapped and her rump slapped sharply and cleanly on the good hard ice.

"Nice going, Mom," muttered the child in her belly.

The cast was white and cold and hard, and not so fine as the winter, but it would be gone in six weeks like the winter, and then the baby would come.

If it should be a girl they would name her Grace Underpressure.

It if should be a boy they would name him Bumby Belmonte. Either way, they would teach the child to fish for the good, clean, icy trout, and it all would be fine.

—Pat Oen

DINNER FOR ONE

▶ ▶ ▶ ▶ ▶ She sat on the end of his bed. She looked tired, but rich.

"I've given you nothing," he said.

"Try not to talk."

She bent forward with the same patient smile he had seen when he woke after the avalanche at Garmisch, and after the bull pinned him to the wall at Dean Witter. The same kindly, destroying smile painted on by her one-armed beautician off Rodeo, the one with the *Guernica* tattoo on her lip.

"Bitch."

"Try not to talk. I shot a chicken. The nurse is bringing some broth."

It was just a scratch and he hadn't bothered putting Bactine on it. He had loved too much and too long, and he was too fast zipping up the pants she had bought him at Fiorucci's in Milan that evening the old Russian died and the Indian howled all night until he died, too. The zipper had been too quick for him, and when he didn't pay attention to the cut, the gangrene had set in.

He knew she wouldn't leave before he got there, but the waiters who had homes to go to would. She had given up everything for him and he had let her. The least he could give her was some finely chopped garlic, the way they had it in Florence the last time he picked up the check.

"I didn't want you to wait."
"They would have held our table."
"Bitch."
"Try not to talk."

She was sitting on his chest now, the way she had after they walked through the fields of opium poppies, and the dung beetle had crawled into his ear.

"I can't breathe."
"Don't be silly."
"I need morphine. Or at least a whiskey."
"We'll have fettucine. You need to keep your strength up."

Then the nurse with the slow, disappointed eyes brought in the clothes they had chosen together at Armando's little shop in Barcelona right before the bomb blew everything to hell. He dressed slowly. Although she wanted to help him, he wouldn't let her.

Outside, a taxi appeared in a sudden clearing in the smog and there was Molo at the wheel. Instead of going home, he turned left and cut across a long line of traffic, and then he knew where they were going, and they wouldn't have to miss their dinner together after all.

"Doctor," she called. "Doctor, come quickly."

But they didn't hear her, and she had to phone Harry's Bar herself to make the reservation for one.

—Martin Russell

To Knot and to Not Knot

▶ ▶ ▶ ▶ ▶ *F*or three days the sea had heaved the old man's boat against the dock like a bad meal. For three days El Pedoviejo had tried to untie his boat, his knuckles bloodied by the barnacles and the ropes and the blood.

It was a good day to untie knots. The wind was like the breath of a dog. The sky was the blue the locals called *azul*. The sea was as wet as that gooey part when you dissect a cow's eye. Now El Pedoviejo reamed his *nariz* with his ancient *dedo*. If he didn't catch a big one soon, the boy would laugh, saying, "Want to borrow my oyster fork?"

He had not caught a fish since 1937. The people of Cacaverde were beginning to mutter that his boat *Malsuerte* was not lucky. "Barnacles are not so bad to eat," he told himself, "but I must bring Barnacle Helper next time."

He could not remember when he had started talking to himself. At first he talked to parts of his body. He would yell, "Knees, are you deaf?" but he received no answer. Now he spoke to the ropes. "Do not be shy, ropes," he sang, "spread yourself like a woman." Still the knots would not budge. El Pedoviejo did not give up. Once he had arm-wrestled a midget for seven days. Being only a simple fisherman, he did not know the midget was using his leg.

In the west the sun hung low. If it were black and white hexagons, he thought, it would look like a soccer ball. He kicked twice toward the sun, hoping the gesture would seem understated yet heroic.

Then, tearing at the knots, he ripped his thumbnail clear back to the elbow. "I wish boy were here," he said softly, "and I was at Harry's Bar. Oh well," he continued with truly unbelievable humility, "at least I do not have a groin pull like the great Earl Campbell of the Oilers of Houston."

It was hard now to see the knots. "The sun has shot his wad of light and fallen spent into the sea," the old man noticed. "Or else it is night." He lay down on the knots, which poked him like a bony woman. He dreamed as always of furry symbols of machismo and freedom. *"Pues,"* he mumbled in his sleep. There is no translation for this word in English.

—Peg Libertus

The Snow Spiraled Down
like Dandruff

▶ ▶ ▶ ▶ ▶ *T*he snow spiraled down like dandruff, flaking the head and shoulders of hatless Angelenos. It was strange weather for L.A.—especially strange for August. The man came into Harry's Bar & American Grill. He shook snowy pearls from his matted hairpiece.

The woman wore leather pants. She twisted around on her stool. It made a noise like stepping on a frog. She looked at the man, oddly. "Dandruff?" she said.

"Nay, but my name is Robert Jordan." He spoke in the pure dialect of bullrings the world over. "I know naught of a sucker called Druff." He looked at the woman, strangely. "Pilaff," he said. *"Qué va?"*

"I am come to seek thee out, *Inglés*."

"And Pablo—*qué va* with that one?"

"Do not speak to me of that mother-*obscenity*. He is of no value. A mortar has divested him of his *obscenities*."

"Both of them?"

"Verdad to tell, he only had the one. For him, the earth will no longer move, *Inglés*."

Robert Jordan ordered martinis, 1,333 parts of gin to 1 of vermouth. He spat an oyster at the spittoon. It missed.

The shiny opalescence put him in mind of the eye of a slaughtered bull, left overlong in the sun. "And what of the girl," he said, "the close-cropped one?"

"Nay, but the earth moved for her twice more, *Inglés*. Then it stopped."

"It is a matter of small wonderment. After forty-two years."

Pilaff looked at me, weirdly. "Shut up, *Inglés*."

"There is naught I can do to aid. My *obscenity obscenity* is not the *obscenity obscenity* of yesteryear."

"Oh, shut up," Pilaff said. "I *obscenity* thee in thy *obscenity*, dog of an *Inglés*."

"I do not provoke," Robert Jordan said.

Outside, the snow continued to fall. It made a soft hissing sound, like butterflies mating.

—Norman Lessing

THE OLD MAN AND THE ROACH

▶ ▶ ▶ ▶ ▶ *I*t was midnight. Or thereabouts. The old man, the one they called Diego, walked into his darkened kitchen and switched on the light. A dozen cockroaches scattered. It reminded him of escaping Nationalists caught in a Loyalist's crossfire.

The old man's good eye caught the frozen form of a straggler. Diego removed his left shoe, slowly. Then, he brought the shoe down swiftly on top of the fleeing roach.

"Cucaracha mugrosa," he screamed as the roach raced across the peeling linoleum and disappeared under the lip of the gas stove.

"I love you, roach, as one of God's creatures, but I will kill you before this night ends," the old man promised. "This one will not raid my humble kitchen again," he thought to himself. As the old man lived alone, he thought to himself a lot. Often, he would think aloud. Too often, his thoughts rambled aimlessly like a school of large fish in a small pond, always bumping into each other. But it was a good life. A widower on a pension. And a *casa con cucarachas.*

The old man saw the antennae sticking out from under the stove top. Nearby lay bread crumbs and a greasy foil cover from a TV dinner. The old man cursed himself silently for not taking his evening meal at Harry's Bar & American Grill. At Harry's there would be no leftovers. He could almost taste the *scampi* as he relished his last visit there. The ambiance was *simpático*. The kitchen, he remembered, was spotless, in a sanitized, stainless steel sort of way.

"The roaches do not run at Harry's," he mused. Roaches. That thought brought back the old man quickly from his musings.

Sensing the old man's distraction, the roach sprang out from under the stove top and raced for the remembered crack in the wall. But the old man had caulked the crack that morning. The *pestito* did not know this. The roach zigged and zagged to confuse the old man. But age had already done that. The old man searched for a new weapon from among his counter utensils. "Not the wooden spoon," he thought. "I must stir my oatmeal with that. The potato peeler? Perhaps. But it does not have enough killing surface," the old man reasoned.

Suddenly, the roached spotted an uncaulked crack in the corner and raced for it. The old man grabbed the nearest piece of paper—his Social Security check—and slammed his eighty-year-old hand down on the roach. Dead.

"Your problems are over, *cucaracha mugrosa,*" the old man sighed. "But there will be others to take your place. This much I know. But that is how it must be. And I will be here waiting. That is how I must be. And so it was. And so it is."

—*Jim Higgins*

IN PARIS THEN YOU COULD WALK
DOWN THE RUE DE CASSEROLE

▶ ▶ ▶ ▶ ▶ *I*n Paris then you could walk down the rue de Casserole to a clean well-lighted café that reminded me of Harry's Bar & American Grill where I had eaten the good *tortellone di magro*. On that morning I found Scott drinking earnestly at the bar.

"You are drinking earnestly," I said.

"No," Scott said, "you drink earnestly. I drink absinthe."

"It is a bad drink," I said. "It will ruin your work."

He grunted like an Indian of my youth. "No," he said, "absinthe makes my art grow sounder."

Later there were ten Indians, and I wrote of them with great dignity.

A tall girl came into the café. She had long legs and small feet.

"You are like a racehorse," I said. I was betting that year.

"Yes," she said. "I am a girl of unbridled passion. Also, I am one of a Lost Generation, and I have no illusions."

"No illusions?"

"It is said that at the time of my birth, I neighed bitterly when the doctor slapped me on the fanny."

We left the café and went to her room and we felt the earth move.

"You are a big two-hearted lover," she said. But afterward I felt the sadness that I did not understand.

In the afternoon I went fishing in the Seine. I fished truly and well, with a long pole and a curved hook, but all I caught that day was an unmentionable condition from the girl of unbridled passion.

"Now I understand the sadness," I thought about a month later. I hobbled in the rain to 61 Boul Yabaise where the old gypsy woman lived.

"It is good to see you again, Papa," she said.

"I am not yet called 'Papa,' " I said, "and if you cannot help me, it is within the realm of possibility that I never will be."

She examined me. "It is nothing for one like you who has the *cojones* of *el toro*. But some day you must die, *Inglés*."

She wishes to provoke you, I thought. But do not provoke. There will always be your work, and the imitations of it, and through them you will live forever.

Or at least as long as there is a Harry's Bar & American Grill.

—*Charles Lansdown*

Well I Suppose I Have
It Coming to Me

Maxwell Perkins
New York, N.Y.

▶ ▶ ▶ ▶ ▶ *D*ear Max,

Well I suppose I have it coming to me and I've already contacted my lawyer but never meant for Gertrude Stein to take off her shirt. The eye is healing swell and it feels good not to feel bad anymore. I guess I owe you the low-down.

I had had a fine meal at Harry's in Florence, starting with a sweet grilled radicchio followed by very nice broiled mussels with herbs and breadcrumbs and polished off with two Tuscan wines. Naturally, I ended up on a stool in Harry's bar with the local *patronos* and was enjoying my third Pernod when John Dos Passos, Gertrude Stein, and Alice B. Toklas walked through the door, creating a buzz among the cognoscenti. Dos Passos was wearing a dark suit and looked like a flatfoot and a short stumpy one to boot. Gertrude, heavy, stout and imposingly dressed in a man's jacket and slacks with short cropped hair led Alice to a table near my spot at the bar. Alice, birdlike and wearing an ugly pillbox hat but rather handsome moustache, looked at me like I was a week's worth of soiled laundry. Dos Passos made a painful spasm as he looked at me but recovered and sat on the next stool and prepared himself for an unpleasant scene.

"Gertrude, Alice, Dos," I drained the Pernod and ordered another. "Ernie, heard you were in town." Dos Passos said this with a thin sneer and a lilt in his body movement which I knew from long experience meant he was going to be insulting. "Read your dispatch from Catalonia. Sure tell the company you're keeping." Now I'm a sonofabitch and have never gotten on with old Dos since the war in Spain and should of kept quiet but didn't and not even sure I'm sorry, even now. "A sissy like you sees the whole war from the Prince Edward suite of the Madrid Hilton and thinks he knows what he's talking about," etc., I sure laid it on. Gertrude interjected: "Hem, you're getting abusive" as she heaved her massive shoulders in my direction. The locals were going mumble-mumble-bitty-bob-bitty-boop and all looking at us. Well, here it goes: I jabbed my finger at old Dos's chest and called him a sissy again. He said I was "insecure" about my masculinity and I wouldn't take that from Freud himself so dared him to bare his chest and show what kind of a man he was, "or don't you have any chest hairs?" Everyone in the bar was tense as hell. "Hem, you have no understanding of true masculinity" (Gertrude, taking off her coat and rolling up her sleeves). Dos balked, said he wouldn't bare his chest unless everyone in the bar followed suit. At that moment we were all standing when

Dos's sweeping gesture caused my fourth Pernod to be knocked over. I was about to pummel him when all eyes turned on Gertrude who was standing too and had taken off her shirt. And all hell broke loose. It all came so quick I don't remember exactly what happened but everyone was pounding on everyone and I got in a few good right crosses (Gertrude decked a sailor with the best return left I ever saw) and somehow Alice got the stuffed Marlin off the wall and was swinging it around and caught me in the face and all went dark and I felt the cool wood floor. Anyway, here I am picking up the pieces with a cake of ice to my eye and sorry about it but not sorry because it was a damn good fight and got a good right fist to Alice before passing out (always wanted to).

Best to you always,
Papa.

—John Geirland

THE GARDEN NEEDS WEEDIN'

▶ ▶ ▶ ▶ *S*pring came in March that year. And the man thought, So this is how it is, this is how it happens, how it always happens, March comes and then it is spring.

And the man, who was eating breakfast, suddenly felt old even though it was only 8:30. He chewed a plain stale bagel and drank *café-sans-lait* and fought an overwhelming sense of *nada*—*nada* milk, *nada* lox, *nada* cream cheese, *nada* Harry's Bar in Toledo. . . .

The woman next door had said, "It is spring," and the truth of that statement had dazzled them both. And the woman who had beauty and money and garden pests had said, "The K Mart ads say that it is time to weed my garden." And the man who had lost twenty-two golf balls and a small dog named Lawrence in the woman's garden knew that it was time. And the woman, who often sighed and said, "Life is like the La Brea Tar Pits," but never explained how, had said, "You will weed my garden?" and she smiled. She was radiant. Her eyes were blue. She flashed a twenty. And the man knew that he would.

And so now the man stood before the garden with the confidence of a man who had once beaten a carnival chicken at ticktacktoe and he saw that the weeds were tall and strong and they were fine and pure in their weediness and not ashamed of being weeds and the man knew that he would have a struggle. He felt the warm sun on his face and he felt strength in his fine brown hands and he thought, So this is how it is, this is how it happens, how it always happens, a man faces his weeds and he faces them in his own way as a man must and he faces them with grace and courage and a pollen mask which makes him look foolish.

The man started his weedeater and he felt its strength as it leaped and jumped with a life of its own like his 3-iron when he sliced. And he began to cut down the weeds where they stood and as they fell he admired them and he felt love for them and he found nine golf balls.

But the man did not know that deep in the garden an army of ants had gathered and they were led by a brave and fearless poodle that they called Larry the Fearless. And now on Larry's command thousands of ants attacked with great courage and fine antlike precision and many brave ants died that day defending their garden home they called Eden after Barbara Eden because "I Dream of Jeannie" was their favorite TV show.

Later, the man and the woman sat in the spring sun drinking demis of Gatorade and they tried to pretend that nothing had happened even though the scent of calamine lotion permeated the air. And the woman who had fine natural-looking blond hair but no tact asked for her twenty back.

And they drank more Gatorade and the woman served sponge cake which came from a box and not from Harry's and they watched "I Dream of Jeannie" and played tick-tacktoe. And the man thought, So this is how it is, this is how it happens, how it always happens, you let her go first and she puts an X in the center square just like the chicken.

But the man won the game with all the Os across the top and the woman sighed, "Life is like the La Brea Tar Pits," but she didn't explain how.

—Gayle Briscoe

ACROSS THE MALL AND
INTO THE WHITE HOUSE

▶ ▶ ▶ ▶ ▶ *T*he President looked at the woman he called Nancy. He knew in his heart that other men had also called her Nancy—it was her name. But he did not wish to think about that now.

They were seated at a table. The table was strong, like wood, but shiny, and not afraid of spilled condiments. Maybe a formica tree was killed for it, the President thought. He looked at it admiringly, for he knew that to kill a formica tree was not an easy thing and required much courage to do the job truly and well. Even with a chainsaw.

"Ron, let's go back to California."

The President drank from his glass. The prune juice was sweet. I have known better prune juice, the President thought, but this prune juice is strong and warm and good and will deliver its message.

"Ron? Are you awake?"

"Yes, beauty. Someday we will go back. Then we will love each other constantly and without hesitation."

The woman smiled. "You hunk. You know what the doctor said about that."

The President saw that the woman he called Nancy was older now than she had been. Time had passed. I hate it when time does that, he thought.

But he and the woman had shared many secrets of life, and she was still able to do marvelous things to his body. The President thought of formica trees, straight and tall.

"If we went to California, we could go to Harry's, you know. You always love Harry's."

"Harry's is very good," the President agreed. "There one can find happiness." And much else that is fine, he thought, although he could not remember what else at the moment. He said, "If you have ever been there you know how it is."

"Dearest, what *are* you talking about? You know I've been there scads of times."

The President finished his prune juice. It tasted fine— like prunes, only more liquidy, which is how it should be when you are with someone you love. The juice was one thing the President truly knew and understood. He wished to speak of it with the woman he called Nancy, whom he still desired when he was not in need of the juice, but she was frightened of rough language. He would speak of it later with Ed, and George, and maybe Gorby.

"We used to have fun here, too," the President said. "At what's-its-name, across the street."

"Oh, Ron. Nobody goes there anymore."

The President knew it was true. When he first came to Washington the food there was very good indeed, but now it was often cold and not tender and made him wish to toss cookies, which he did not enjoy, although at one time even that was good.

Rain began to fall. It fell as it always had, downward and in little drops, but the President did not notice, because he was inside.

—*Daniel R. White*

The
Trophy
Room

▼

PRIZE HEMINGWAY PARODIES
FROM THE PAST

ACROSS THE STREET
AND INTO THE GRILL

▶ ▶ ▶ ▶ ▶ *T*his is my last and best and true and only meal, thought Mr. Perley as he descended at noon and swung east on the beat-up sidewalk of Forty-fifth Street. Just ahead of him was the girl from the reception desk. I am a little fleshed up around the crook of the elbow, thought Perley, but I commute good.

He quickened his step to overtake her and felt the pain again. What a stinking trade it is, he thought. But after what I've done to other assistant treasurers, I can't hate anybody. Sixteen deads, and I don't know how many possibles.

The girl was near enough now so he could smell her fresh receptiveness, and the lint in her hair. Her skin was light blue, like the sides of horses.

"I love you," he said, "and we are going to lunch together for the first and only time, and I love you very much."

"Hello, Mr. Perley," she said, overtaken. "Let's not think of anything."

A pair of fantails flew over from the sad old Guaranty Trust Company, their wings set for a landing. A lovely double, thought Perley, as he pulled. "Shall we go to the Hotel Biltmore, on Vanderbilt Avenue, which is merely a feeder lane for the great streets, or shall we go to Schrafft's, where my old friend Botticelli is captain of girls and where they have the mayonnaise in fiascos?"

"Let's go to Schrafft's," said the girl, low. "But first I must phone Mummy." She stepped into a public booth and dialed true and well, using her finger. Then she telephoned.

As they walked on, she smelled good. She smells good, thought Perley. But that's all right, I add good. And when we get to Schrafft's, I'll order from the menu, which I like very much indeed.

They entered the restaurant. The wind was still west, ruffling the edges of the cookies. In the elevator, Perley took the controls. "I'll run it," he said to the operator. "I checked out long ago." He stopped true at the third floor, and they stepped off into the men's grill.

"Good morning, my Assistant Treasurer," said Botticelli, coming forward with a fiasco in each hand. He nodded at the girl, who he knew was from the West Seventies and whom he desired.

"Can you drink the water here?" asked Perley. He had the fur trapper's eye and took in the room at a glance, noting that there was one empty table and three pretty waitresses.

Botticelli led the way to the table in the corner, where Perley's flanks would be covered.

"Alexanders," said Perley. "Eighty-six to one. The way Chris mixes them. Is this table all right, Daughter?"

Botticelli disappeared and returned soon, carrying the old Indian blanket.

"That's the same blanket, isn't it?" asked Perley.

"Yes. To keep the wind off," said the Captain, smiling from the backs of his eyes. "It's still west. It should bring the ducks in tomorrow, the chef thinks."

Mr. Perley and the girl from the reception desk crawled down under the table and pulled the Indian blanket over them so it was solid and good and covered them right. The girl put her hand on his wallet. It was cracked and old and held his commutation book. "We are having fun, aren't we?" she asked.

"Yes, Sister," he said.

"I have here the soft-shelled crabs, my Assistant Treasurer," said Botticelli. "And another fiasco of the 1926. This one is cold."

"Dee the soft-shelled crabs," said Perley from under the blanket. He put his arm around the receptionist good.

"Do you think we should have a green pokeweed salad?" she asked. "Or shall we not think of anything for a while?"

"We shall not think of anything for a while, and Botticelli would bring the pokeweed if there was any," said Perley. "It isn't the season." Then he spoke to the Captain. "Botticelli, do you remember when we took all the mailing envelopes from the stockroom, spit on the flaps, and then drank rubber cement till the foot soldiers arrived?"

"I remember, my Assistant Treasurer," said the Captain. It was a little joke they had.

"He used to mimeograph pretty good," said Perley to the girl. "But that was another war. Do I bore you, Mother?"

"Please keep telling me about your business experiences, but not the rough parts." She touched his hand where the knuckles were scarred and stained by so many old mimeographings. "Are both your flanks covered, my dearest?" she asked, plucking at the blanket. They felt the Alexanders in their eyeballs. Eighty-six to one.

"Schrafft's is a good place and we're having fun and I love you," Perley said. He took another swallow of the 1926, and it was a good and careful swallow. "The stockroom men were very brave," he said, "but it is a position where it is extremely difficult to stay alive. Just outside that room there is a little bare-assed highboy and it is in the way of the stuff that is being brought up. The hell with it. When you make a breakthrough, Daughter, first you clean out the baskets and the halfwits, and all the time they have the fire escapes taped. They also shell you with old production orders, many of them approved by the general manager in charge of sales. I am boring you and I will not at this time discuss the general manager in charge of sales as we are unquestionably being listened to by that waitress over there who is setting out the decoys."

"I am going to give you my piano," the girl said, "so that when you look at it you can think of me. It will be something between us."

"Call up and have them bring the piano to the restaurant," said Perley. "Another fiasco, Botticelli!"

They drank the sauce. When the piano came, it wouldn't play. The keys were stuck good. "Never mind, we'll leave it here, Cousin," said Perley.

They came out from under the blanket and Perley tipped their waitress exactly fifteen percent minus withholding. They left the piano in the restaurant, and when they went down the elevator and out and turned in to the old, hard, beat-up pavement of Fifth Avenue and headed south toward Forty-fifth Street, where the pigeons were, the air was as clean as your grandfather's howitzer. The wind was still west.

I commute good, thought Perley, looking at his watch. And he felt the old pain of going back to Scarsdale again.

—E. B. White

For Whom the Gong Sounds

▶ ▶ ▶ ▶ ▶ *R*obert Jordan snapped the lock of his revolver, made certain the machine gun at his hip was handy, gripped his *máquina* and continued to crawl up the Guadarrama hills on his belly. Robert Jordan grinned. You're almost there, he told himself. He'd been telling himself things like that all day. Robert Jordan was hunching over a rocky ledge now, hanging on by the bristles of his chest. The warm Spanish earth scraped his belly. Robert Jordan could feel a pine cone in his navel. It was a resinous pine cone, the kind they grow in Catalonia. These people, Robert Jordan thought, turn out to be people. There's no getting away from that. Sure there isn't. Hell, no.

A gypsy was sitting on a rock strumming a guitar. With one bare foot he practiced range-finding with a submachine gun. The other foot lay idly on his *máquina*. The gypsy's face was the color of old Virginia ham.

"*Salud,*" Robert Jordan said.

Fernando eyed him through the barrel of a Lewis gun. Robert Jordan made certain his Mauser was uncocked. The gypsy's voice was like golden Amontillado gurgling out of a wineskin.

"Thou wast of the streetcar, *camarada?*"

"*Cómo no?* Why not?" Robert Jordan thought of the last streetcar he had blown up. They had found arms and legs all over the roofs. One femur had gone as far as Valladolid.

"*Quién sabe,*" said Jacinto. "Who knows."

"Each according to each," said Ignacio. "Street cars I have a boredom of. We have heard what we have heard. *Sí.* Yes." He flung some hand grenades into a nose bag, trampling them firmly with his rope-soled feet.

"*Hombre,*" said Anselmo, squinting down the barrel of a 45-mm gun. "One goes to the cave."

"*Bueno,*" said Robert Jordan. "Good."

Robert Jordan and the gypsy continued to scrabble up the hill past a deserted sawmill. Juanito burrowed his way, Andalusian fashion, into a pile of sawdust, and emerged after a little while, grinning sweatily. Robert Jordan opened his pack, making sure that all was as it had been. He unlocked the grommet, untied the drawstrings, uncoiled the insulating wire and tossed the caber. His groping fingers came in reassuring contact with a bunch of bayonets. His automatic pistols were safe, so were the hand grenades, the old French '75 and his father's sawed-off shotgun. His father had been a preacher, a man of God in Ohio. He drew forth a bottle of TNT and a quart of Haig and Haig. It might come in handy when the time came for blowing up the boardwalk. He studied the bottle of Haig and Haig and thought, no. They'll take me for a fascist. A bloody fascist, that's what they'll take me for. He put the bottle of Haig and Haig back into the bandolier of ammunition, screwing it down with a grenade pin, a belaying pin and a Skull and

Bones pin. Then he got out a magnum of Courvoisier. This is more their stuff, he said to himself. Then to make sure, he pulled out a carton of Abdullas and a box of Corona Coronas. That was all he had in his knapsack except, of course, his sleeping bag, a case of Old Grandad, three pairs of rope-soled shoes and an asbestos suit for when he blew up the boardwalk.

An old man sat at the mouth of the cave guarding the entrance with a Mauser, a Howitzer, a Winchester and a flyswatter.

"Salud, camarada," said the old man.

"Equally," said Robert Jordan, then added, *"Hola!"* for good measure.

"Thou. Thou was of the streetcar?"

"Wast."

He is old, Robert Jordan said to himself. And the gypsy is old too, and some day I will be old. But I'm not old yet, not yet, I'm not old.

"He knows of which whereof he speaks of, old one," the gypsy was saying.

"Qué va, young one."

"It makes well to joke, old one."

"Pass, middle-aged one."

The mouth of the cave was camouflaged by a curtain of saddle blankets, matadors' capes and the soles of old es-padrilles. Inside it smelt of man-sweat, acrid and brown ... horse-sweat and magenta. There was the leathery smell of leather and the coppery smell of copper and borne in on the clear night air came the distant smell of skunk.

The wife of Pablo was stirring *frijoles* in a Catalonian wineskin. She wore rope-soled shoes and a belt of hand grenades. Over her magnificent buttocks swung a sixteenth-century cannon taken from the Escorial.

"I *obscenity* in the *obscenity* of thy *unprintable obscenity,*" said Pilar.

"This is the *Inglés* of the streetcar. He of the boardwalk to come soon."

"I *obscenity* in the *unprintable* of the milk of all streetcars." The woman was stirring the steaming mess with the horns of a Mura bull. She stared at Robert Jordan then smiled. *"Obscenity, obscenity, obscenity,"* she said, not unkindly.

"Qué va," said Robert Jordan. *"Bueno.* Good."

"Menos mal," said El Sordo. "Not so good."

"Go *unprint* thyself," said Pilar. The gypsy went outside and *unprinted* himself.

The girl with the shaved head filled a tin pail full of petite marmite and handed it to him and she gave him a great swig from the wineskin and he chewed the succulent bits of horsemeat and they said nothing.

And now Esteban stood beside him on the rim of the gorge. This is it, Robert Jordan said to himself. I believe this is it. I did not think it was this to be it but it seems to be it, alright. Robert Jordan spat down the gorge. Pablo watched the fast disappearing globule of man-saliva then slowly, softly spat down the gorge. Pilar said *obscenity* thy saliva then she too spat down the gorge. This time it was Pablo's gorge.

The girl was walking beside him.

"Hola, Inglés," she said. "Hello, English."

"Equally, *guapa,*" said Robert Jordan.

"Qué va," said the girl.

"Rabbit."

Robert Jordan pulled the pistol lanyard up, cocked his *máquina* and tightened the ropes of his rope-soled shoes.

"Vamos," he said. "Let's go."

"Sí," said Maria. "Yes."

They walked on in silence until they came to a rocky ledge. There were rough rocks and thistles and a wild growth of Spanish dagger. Robert Jordan spread his buffalo robe out for himself and allowed Maria to lie near him on a bed of nettles. The earth moved.

"Rabbit," said Robert Jordan. "Hast aught?"

"Nay, naught."

"Maria," he said. "Mary. Little shaved head."

"Let me go with thee and be thy rabbit."

The earth moved again. This time it was a regular earthquake. Californians would have called it a temblor.

Robert Jordan had reached the boardwalk. He lay in the gorse and rubble. He had his infernal machine beside him, some hand grenades, a blunderbuss, an arquebus and a greyhound bus. His *máquina* was held securely in his teeth. Across the ravine Anselmo was snipping off sentries as they passed.

Listen, Robert Jordan said to himself, only the fascist bombs made so much noise he couldn't hear. You had to do what you did. If you don't do what you do now you'll never do what you do now. Now now you won't. Sure it does. He lashed the wire through the rings of the cotter pins of the release levers of the wires of the main spring of the coil, insulating it with a piece cut off the bottom of his rope-soled shoes.

What about the others . . . Eladio and Ignacio . . . Anselmo and St. Elmo? And Rabbit? I wonder how Rabbit is? Stop that now. This is no time to think about Rabbit . . . or rabbits. Better think about something else. Think about llamas. It's better to breathe, he thought. It's always much better to breathe. Sure it is. The time was gradually, inevitably drawing near. Someone in the valley was singing an old Catalonian song. A plane crashed quietly overhead. Robert Jordan lay still and listened for the gong to sound.

—*Cornelia Otis Skinner*

THE SNOWS OF STUDIOFIFTYFOUR*

Studiofiftyfour, a converted movie theater fifty-seven feet above sea level, was said to have been the liveliest discotheque in New York City. Close to the top seats in the balcony was discovered a matchbook cover[1] bearing the White House seal. No one knows what the White House aide was seeking at that altitude.

▶ ▶ ▶ ▶ ▶ It was morning, and had been morning for some time, and he was waiting for the plane. It was difficult to speak.

"Can you see all right?" the attendant from the Fat Farm asked as they approached the ticket counter.

---

*The concept here is that Truman Capote, having difficulty finishing his Proustian epic *Answered Prayers*, resorts to another's style to break his writer's block—much as a stutterer can often speak lucidly using a different accent. Thus we have the unlikely combination of Capote's sensibility melded into Hemingway's style.

[1]"Snows," in this case, apparently refers not to the material that falls on mountains, but to a white powder that is arranged in a thin line by such a pusher as a matchbook cover and is then ingested up a straw into either nostril—a practice referred to as "snorting."

"It's okay unless the bandages slip," he said. "Then it's all fuzzy."

"How do you feel?"

"A little wobbly."

"Does it hurt?"

"Only when I sit down."

He thought about the railway station at Karabük and the head-light of the Simplon–Orient cutting the dark now, and he thought about his enemies and how he wished he had them laid out across the tracks. They would make a long row. Perhaps a mile. Too many, maybe. But he had fought often, and they had always picked the finest places to have the fights. The tea place in the Plaza Hotel with the palms. The El Morocco with the zebra stripes. The Bistro in Beverly Hills. That was where Jerry Zipkin[2] came out of the dark restaurant gloom that time, blinking his eyes, and he had hit him right along the chops, twice, hard, and when the Social Moth— that was what Johnny Fairchild called him, wasn't it, old cock?— didn't go down he knew he was in a fight.

He wished it had been at El Morocco, which was a good place to fight, with the palm trees and the high ground off the dance floor where the band played.

"Do you have any bags to check?"

He came to with a start. The gauze head-bandages from the face-lift had slipped down on one side.

---

[2]A familiar social figure of the times, in later years referred to as the "Social Moth" for criticizing a party to which he had not been invited in front of a man who turned out to be the host and who threw Zipkin down a staircase, at the foot of which he was caught by Nan Kempner, one of the great beauties and Zipkin-catchers of the day.

"I'm sorry about the one eye," he said. "But I have two bags. I will carry the smaller on board."

"All right," the flight clerk said. He was a fine desk clerk with high cheekbones and a plastic identification badge. He had good hands, too, and it was with pleasure that through the one good eyehole he watched the clerk tie the baggage check to the handle of the big Vuitton with one hand, as it was supposed to be done if the bag was to be dominated properly, with the good brusque motion of the *recorte* and the baggage check truly fixed. He thought about the baggage itself, jiggling down the conveyor belt, and how it would disappear through the leather straps that hung down like a portcullis and maybe he would see the bag again at the LaGuardia. The LaGuardia was not the same since they had built the rust-colored parking building that obscured the view from the Grand Central Parkway, but then we were not the same either. He would miss the bag if it did not turn up at the LaGuardia, and went instead to the Logan, which was in Massachusetts and had the fogs. He would sorely be troubled if the bag went to the Logan. He had always packed a neat bag. It was a fine experience to open the bag up in the hotel room and see everything laid out just the way he had packed it, with the knuckle-dusters next to the big Christmas stocking he liked to hang at the foot of the bed.

"Smoking or nonsmoking?" the flight clerk asked him. He answered through the bandages. He asked for a window seat. Just then it occurred to him that when the stewardess came by with the tray of steamed towels and the tongs to grip them, which was what he truly liked about first class, he could not use the fine hot face towels because of the bandages on his face. It came with a rush; not as a rush of water or of wind; but of a sudden evil-smelling emptiness.

He thought about being alone in the motel room in Akron with the big table lamps, having quarreled in Memphis, and how he had started his enemies list, and how long it was, and how he had used the Dewey decimal system to arrange it in the green calfskin notebooks. Under K there was Stanley Kauffmann, who had written forty unproduced plays and ten unpublished novels, which had wrecked him just about as much as any other thing had wrecked him, but it did not stop him from trying to wreck people who were writing true stories about Christmas in Alabama and how they hung the mule from the rafters. And Tynan, under T, Kenneth Tynan,[3] who had worn the same seersucker overcoat since the year the dwarfs came out on the Manzanares along the Prado road, and who wrote snide about his party in the Plaza where John Kenneth Galbraith[4] had danced the Turkey Trot. Under A, he had Dick Avedon, who had hung snide two portraits of him in the exhibition that had him young in the first and like an old goat in the other. He thought how good the notebooks felt to the touch, and how he could buy fill-ins at Cartier when the lists became too long, and how he could look in them when the time came. Vengeance went in pairs, on roller skates, and moved absolutely silently on the pavements.

He looked through the eyehole of his bandages at the standbys. They would begin to call them soon enough, and

---

[3] A drama critic and essayist whose work often appeared in *The New Yorker*.

[4] A tall cranelike economist of the times who espoused the curious Keynesian theory that it is better to set high prices than to pay them.

some of them would sit in coach. He had sat in coach once. But that was when he was beginning as a writer, and now that he was successful he liked the face towels and the tongs to grip them, and the crêpes with shrimp within and the tall green bottles of California Pinot and the seats that went back when you pushed the button. They had the buttons in coach but they did not have the hot towels and the other things. So when the time came and he had to work the fat off his soul and body, the way a fighter went into the mountains to work and train and burn it out, he didn't go into coach. He went to the Fat Farm where they took his face and lifted it, and took a tuck in his behind as well, and they put the bandages on afterward. The sprinklers washed the grass early in the morning and the doctors had taken his vodka martinis away from him, and later on, up in the room, they took the cheese away from him, too.

He thought about the people in the notebooks he wished were not there. He wrote things simply and truly that he had heard at the dinner tables when he sat with the very social and listened with the total recall that was either 94.6 or 96.8 percent, he never could remember which. They did not understand him when he wrote about this and wrote about what they talked about at the Côte Basque. So they cut him: Slim Keith, Mariella Agnelli, Pamela Harriman, Gloria Vanderbilt, Gloria Guinness, and so did Babe Paley, whom he loved and who called him "daughter." He knew he would never be invited to dine with Mr. Paley under the great tiger painting at the polished table which reflected the underside of the silverware. He tried not to think about that. You had to be equipped with good insides so that you did not go to pieces over such things. It was better to remember that the difference about the very social was that they were all very treacherous. Almost as treacherous as the very gauche were boring. They played too much backgammon. Lee Radziwill! The Princess, who looked fine in jodhpurs, although she never wore them that he could remember at the backgammon table, had a fine nose and a whispery way of talking. She had told him how Arthur Schlesinger had thrown Gore Vidal out of the White House onto Pennsylvania Avenue, which was the length of two football fields away from the front steps, a long toss for anyone, but which was logical enough if you knew what a great arm Schlesinger had and how he had gripped Vidal by the laces and spiraled him. He had remembered because it was a good story, and it told about Arthur Schlesinger's great arm and the proper way to grip Vidal if you had to throw him a long distance. So he had told the story in an interview in Playgirl *which was not as good a publication as* Der Querschnitt *or the* Frankfurter Zeitung, *but had a substantial number of readers anyway, and so Vidal sued him. The Princess did not support him. She said she could not remember telling him such a thing, which meant that she was treacherous, either that, or that she had a recall of .05 or 1.6, he couldn't decide which, which was not a great talent. He decided he would not take her to Schruns that Christmas where the snow, which he had never skied, was so bright it hurt your eyes when you looked out from the* Weinstube.

He hoped there would not be three nuns on the plane. That had been a superstition he had held to for as long as he could remember. It was involuntary, but then he was not a complete man. It was an inconvenience also. You could not dictate to the airlines not to seat three nuns. Once on his way by air to the chalet in Gstaad he had looked through the curtain into coach and three nuns were sitting in a row and he had called out, "Nuns! Nuns! Three nuns in coach!" It spoiled everything about that trip, but he knew he could not brawl with three nuns and ask them to defenestrate, even though they were over the Kaiser-Jägers at the time which had the sawmill and the valley above where it was a good place to walk the bulldog. Brawling with nuns was not part of the code by which he lived. Besides, if the nuns fought, the odds were three to one, and maybe more if the bishops sitting behind the nuns involved themselves.

He thought about the very rich, who were just the same as him, and how his talent started to erode. Perhaps it was because of the negrinos, and the cherry-pit taste of the good kirsch, and the margaritas with the salt around the rims, and the cool glasses of Tab the color of the Dese River above Noghera where the sails of the sailing barges moved through the countryside for Venice where off the Lido Beach he had sat on the bicycle paddle-boat with C. Z. Guest[5] and told wicked stories to her about C. Z. Guest. He could no longer write these wicked tales because he had the block, the writer's block, which with a wide snout like a hyena's, like death, had come and rested its head on his nice little Olivetti, and he could smell its breath. He had tried to send it away. He thought he would write about the great fights if the breath no longer dom-

---

[5]One of the famous Cochrane sisters of Boston who among other things danced in the chorus of the Ziegfeld Follies before becoming a successful syndicated gardening columnist.

inated the Olivetti. About the Hemingway fight with Max Eastman over the chest hair in the office of Max Perkins, who always wore his hat indoors and had the sweet smile. Or maybe he could write about the time F. Scott Fitzgerald fought the six Argentinians. He would write about the zebra cushions of El Morocco where Humphrey Bogart had fought over the big stuffed panda that they had tried to take away from him, coming for the panda steadily and lumpily past the linen-clothed tables with the single roses in their thin vases, and the hatcheck girl had cried like a girl. He had once arm-wrestled with Bogart on the set of Beat the Devil and he had won that one although Bogart had said, "Sweetheart, you wouldn't do this to an old character actor." He was very strong in the upper chest then, and still was, and he could pick up the front end of a Hillman Minx off a child with the best of them. He wanted to write about the night that Norman Mailer had hit Gore Vidal in the eye at Lally Weymouth's salon—the evening that Vidal had called "the night of the tiny fist." There had been the good remarks. Was it not Christopher Morley who said that a literary movement is two authors in town who hate each other? Was it not Robert Browning who had described Swinburne as a monkey creature "who sat in a sewer and added to it"? Ayee, that was fine. He himself had called Jack Kerouac a "typist," which was clever but he was not sure it compared and maybe it would not get into Bartlett's Quotations.

The writer's block moved a little closer. It crouched now, heavier, so that he could hardly breathe.

"You've got a hell of a breath," he told it.

It had no shape. It simply occupied space.

"Get off my Olivetti," he said.

And then the flight attendant said, "Will all those holding blue *boarding passes board the plane," and the weight went from his chest, and suddenly it was all right.*

It was difficult to get him into the plane because of what they had done to him in the Fat Farm operating room, but once in he lay back in the seat and they eased a cushion under him. He winced when the plane swung around and with one last bump rose and he saw the staff, some of them, waving, and the Fat Farm beside the hill, flattening out as they rose. He tried not to think about the hot towels and the tongs. He remembered that he was a new man again, his face lifted and perky as a jackal's under the bandages and his rear end tucked up and river-smooth. They had drawn him true and taut, so that his skin was as drumhead tight as the tuna's he had caught at Key West and eaten with long-tipped asparagus and a glass of Sancerre with Tennessee Williams sitting opposite. *Qué tal?* Tennessee, and he wished he had been named after a state, too, perhaps South Dakota, or Utah even, and not with a name shared with that peppery man who sold suits in Kansas City.

The plane began to climb and they were going to the East it seemed. They were in a storm, the rain as thick as if they were flying through a waterfall, and then they were out, and through the plane window he suddenly saw the great, high, shadow-pocked cathedral of Studiofiftyfour with the mothlike forms dancing, the hands clapping overhead, and the bare-chested sweepers, who built up their crotches with handkerchiefs, sweeping up the old poppers with long-handled brooms. And then he knew that this was where he was going. He thought about the smooth leather of the banquettes under his rear end and how he would look out and think about his enemies. We will have some good destruction, he thought.

—*George Plimpton*

We Were in a Back-House
in Juan-les-Pins

▶ ▶ ▶ ▶ ▶ *W*e were in a back-house in Juan-les-Pins. Bill had lost controll of his splincter muscles. There were wet *Matins* in the rack beside the door. There were wet *Eclairers de Nice* in the rack over his head. When the King of Bulgeria came in Bill was just firing a burst that struck the old limeshit twenty feet down with a *splat-tap*. All the rest came just like that. The King of Bulgaria began to whirl round and round.

"The great thing in these affairs—" he said.

Soon he was whirling faster and faster. Then he was dead.

—*F. Scott Fitzgerald*

Beer in the Sergeant-Major's Hat
(Or, The Sun Also Sneezes)

▶ ▶ ▶ ▶ ▶ *H*ank went into the bathroom to brush his teeth.

"The hell with it," he said. "She shouldn't have done it."

It was a good bathroom. It was small and the green enamel was peeling off the walls. But the hell with that, as Napoleon said when they told him Josephine waited without. The bathroom had a wide window through which Hank looked at the pines and larches. They dripped with a faint rain. They looked smooth and comfortable.

"The hell with it," Hank said. "She shouldn't have done it."

He opened the cabinet over the washbasin and took out his toothpaste. He looked at his teeth in the mirror. They were large yellow teeth, but sound. Hank could still bite his way for a while.

Hank unscrewed the top of the toothpaste tube, thinking of the day when he had unscrewed the lid of the coffee jar, down on the Pukayuk River, when he was trout fishing. There had been larches there too. It was a damn good river, and the trout had been damn good trout. They liked being hooked. Everything had been good except the coffee, which had been lousy. He had made it Watson's way, boiling it for two hours and a half in his knapsack. It had tasted like hell. It had tasted like the socks of the Forgotten Man.

"She shouldn't have done it," Hank said out loud. Then he was silent.

Hank put the toothpaste down and looked around. There was a bottle of alcohol on top of the built-in drawers where the towels were kept. It was grain alcohol. Velma hated rubbing alcohol with its harsh irritants. Her skin was sensitive. She hated almost everything. That was because she was sensitive. Hank picked up the bottle of alcohol, pulled the cork out, and smelled it. It had a damn good smell. He poured some alcohol into this tooth glass and added some water. Then the alcohol was all misty, with little moving lines in it, like tiny ripples coming to the surface. Only they didn't come to the surface. They just stayed in the alcohol, like goldfish in a bowl.

Hank drank the alcohol and water. It had a warm sweetish taste. It was warm all the way down. It was warm as hell. It was warmer than whiskey. It was warmer than that Asti Spumante they had that time in Capozzo when Hank was with the Arditi. They had been carp fishing with landing nets. It had been a good day. After the fourth bottle of Asti Spumante Hank fell into the river and came out with his hair full of carp. Old Peguzzi laughed until his boots rattled on the hard gray rock. And afterward Peguzzi got gonorrhoea on the Piave. It was a hell of a war.

Hank poured more alcohol into the glass and added less water. He drank solemnly, liking his face in the mirror. It was warm and a bit shiny. His eyes had a kind of fat glitter. They were large pale blue eyes, except when he was mad. Then they were dark blue. When he had a good edge on they were almost gray. They were damn good eyes.

"The hell with it," he said. "She shouldn't have done it."

He poured more alcohol into the glass and added a little water—very little. He raised the glass in a toast to his face in the mirror.

"Gentlemen, I give you alcohol. Not, gentlemen, because I cannot give you wine or whiskey, but because I desire to cultivate in you the fundamental art of intoxication. The alcohol drinker, gentlemen, is the hair-shirt drinker. He likes his penance strong."

Hank drained the glass and refilled it. The bottle was nearly empty now, but there was more alcohol in the cellar. It was a good cellar, and there was plenty of alcohol in it.

"Gentlemen," Hank said, "when I was with Napoleon at Solferino we drank cognac. When I was with Moore at Coruña we drank port with a dash of brandy. It was damn good port, and Moore was a damn good drinker. When I was with Kitchener at Khartoum we drank the stale of horses. With Kuroki on the Yalu I drank saki, and with Byng at Arras I drank Scotch. These, gentlemen, were drinks of diverse charms. Now that I am with you, gentlemen, we shall drink alcohol, because alcohol is the Holy Mother of all drinking."

Hank's face in the mirror wavered like a face behind thin smoke. It was a face drawn on gray silk by unscrupulous shadows. It was not a face at all. Hank scowled at it. The reflected scowl was as merciless as an earthquake.

"The hell with it," he said. "She shouldn't have done it."

He leaned against the washbowl and squeezed some toothpaste on his toothbrush. It was a long toothbrush, about six feet long. It was springy, like a trout rod. Hank brought his elbow around with a sweep and spread some toothpaste on his upper lip. He supported himself with both hands and squinted at his reflection.

"The white moustache, gentlemen," he burbled. "The mark of a goddamn ambassador."

Hank drank the rest of the alcohol straight. For a moment his stomach came up between his ears. But that passed and he only felt as if he had been bitten in the back of the neck by a tiger.

"Not by a damn sight she shouldn't," he said.

With large gestures he applied toothpaste to his eyebrows and temples.

"Not a complete work, gentlemen," he yelled. "Just an indication of what can be done. And now for a brief moment I leave you. While I am gone let your conversation be clean."

Hank stumbled down to the living-room. It seemed a long way to the cellar where the alcohol was. There were steps to go down. The hell with the steps.

The cat was sleeping in a tight curve on the carpet.

"Jeeze Christ," Hank said. " 'At's a hell of a fine cat."

It was a large black cat with long fur. It was a cat a guy could get on with. Jeeze Christ, yes. Hank lay down on the floor and put his head on the cat. The cat licked at the toothpaste on Hank's eyebrow. Then it sneezed and bit his ear.

"Jeeze Christ," Hank said. "The hell with it. She shouldn't have done it."

He slept.

—*Raymond Chandler*

OVER THE RIVER
AND THROUGH THE WOODS

I

▶ ▶ ▶ ▶ ▶ *W*hen the shooting stopped, I needed a drink. Do not think I needed a drink because I was afraid. I have been afraid several times, but never because of the shooting. I needed a drink because I was thirsty.

I took a pull from the bottle. The whiskey was good. It burned my mouth and felt good and warm going down my esophagus and into my stomach. From there it was digested, and went to my kidneys and my bladder and into my intestines, and was good.

Then I got up from the ditch and walked back to the Red Cross truck. The doctor was bandaging someone's groin. It looked bad.

"What's your problem?" he asked me.

"I've been hit," I said.

"Where?"

"Here."

"Let's see. Hmm."

"Is it bad?"

"Nipped the left ventricle."

"Damn."

He bandaged my heart and I got a three-week furlough. I decided to go to Paris and I went to Paris. I had not been to Paris since I had left it, and it was fine to be back. I walked down the rue Pensées, and turned off at the rue J'Accuse. On the rue François-Hardy was a café. I did not want to go inside it. It looked dirty, and poorly lighted. But I saw Lady Bob Ashton and her fiancé Steve inside, so I went in. Bob had sleek curves like a high-powered hunting bow, and her sweater held them very well.

"Hullo, Abe," Bob said. "Hullo."

"Hello, Bob. Hello, Steve."

"Hello, Abe. Join us?" Steve motioned for me to sit down. "I was just telling Bob what a splendid time we are going to have in San Cugat."

"Oh, rather. I say, Abe, we *are* going to have a fine time," Bob said. She put a cigar in her mouth. "Give a chap a light?"

"I say, Abe, why don't you come along?" Steve asked. "You can come with us on the train, and we'll do a bit of fishing. Oh, do come. Do."

"Buy a pint of beer?" Bob asked. I think she was tight. "Have a glass of wine? Drink a pint a milk a day?"

"You're tight."

"Don't talk like a fool."

"You're cock-eyed."

"Oh, give a chap a break."

"I say, don't, what?"

"What?"

"What?"

"What?"

"I said, I say, don't, what? What?"

"Will I not!"

"I say, do don't."

"What?"

"I say, do let's don't. Do. Don't."

"Oh, rather."

"What?"

"What?"

II

That night I walked along the rue Petit-Mal. I must have been tight, because my mind was jumping around, and I felt pretty rotten. I thought about Bob. I had met her at an Italian field hospital for anti-fascist bullfighters. I crossed the Pont Pilate and walked up the rue Nausée. I had told Bob about everything. I told her about the time I was a boy in Minnesota. I had been present when my father had tried to deliver an Indian baby with a can-opener and a copy of *A Sportsman's Sketches* by Turgenev. It had been bad. The Indian father had cut his throat with the book, and the mother had gone blind reading the can-opener. Well, that was all past. And Bob was such a swell friend. Oh yes, a swell friend. The hell she was!

I passed several poules lying in the street, but walked over them. I had a few drinks at a café on the rue Mauvaise-Foi, and arm-wrestled with a Cuban fisherman. "I have been fishing the *obscenity* big fish today," he said. He beat me, and suddenly I started to cry, and felt like hell. The old fisherman patted me on the back. "There, there," he said. "It is nothing. When thou hast lived much like I have, thou knowest that it is nothing. I was a soldier in the war. I have lived much. It is nothing."

I asked him what he did in the war.

"I was twenty-one years of old. By myself alone, with a single hand. I defeated a group of Spanish soldiers. They were disguised as a machine for thrashing the wheat, but I was not fooled. I have many scars." He took off his clothes and showed me his scars. They were all over his body. "Also, I lose both the eyes." He took off his glasses, and I saw his eyes. Moisture beaded on the glass. "Also the hair falls out, I lose the power of the sex. The hands turn into claws, I have no heart, my head is stuffed with straw, and I am talking to you through the aid of a ventriloquist." He bought me a drink. After we had drunk the whiskey he said, "So thou seest, my friend, because I have lived much I know how to have a good time." I shook his hand, and he left.

Then I walked back to the hotel, and went to my good room. I slipped my shoes off and went to sleep. Later that night, I woke up and heard the wind howling and the rain beating against the windows. It felt good to be warm and asleep under the blankets. One of the blankets was my favorite pink frilly flannel comforter with the blue bunny rabbits on it, and it felt very, very good.

III

The next day I met Bob and Steve at the Gare Eau Way, and we got a train for San Cugat. It was a good day, and we had good riding. Bob looked damned good. She wore her hair brushed back like a boy's and a man's hat and jacket, and a beard. Once we were alone in the compartment, I held her close to me and kissed her. Her eyes looked all the way into mine. She said, "Oh, don't!" and pulled away. I didn't. Then I sat back and thought about the war.

Oh yes, the war. Here's to you, war. I remembered the last battle I had been in. It had been bad. We had spent many nights in the foothills when Franco's men besieged our camp. The fascists had sent a large number of troops across the lake disguised as crippled mules. I watched them through the trees, stepping out of the mules' skins and washing each other of the blood and tissue. We had been pinned down, and were surrounded without food or water for three weeks. I had decided not to wait them out. I didn't mind. You paid for everything in life. It was a simple exchange of values. So I stood up and shot as many men as I could, the bullets cutting deep into the soldiers' muscle and bone, and lodging there with a good clean pain. Many of the men screamed and died. The sun was hot, and there had been good screaming and good dying. I threw the mule skins into the river, and with some of the leftover mule meat made a fine casserole. Then I waited behind a rock until the others died of boredom. That had been good, damned good.

"I say, bungo old sportbean chap old man old thing, Abe

old classmate fellow bean. We're here." Steve said. We had arrived at San Cugat. We took a taxi to the hotel, and we each had a good small room and a nice bed and a glass of milk and a cookie.

IV

The next day Steve and I went fishing while Bob walked around the town. I bought four twelve-liter bottles of wine from a small shop that smelled of wine and liters, and we packed our gear and set off.

We arrived at the river, and Steve went upstream to fish flies. I stayed downstream to fish fish. I baited my line and waded out into the cold stream. Ahead of me there were woods, and a forest. There were trees extending north and south, and pine scrub birch timbertops to the left of a ravine. Down a canyon ran a ridge of maple log peatmoss bog bark, while just above the left of the front of the mountain face was a cliff of ravine-bottomed dune boulders and a gush of mulch leaves streaming through a gulley patch as a deer of goats ran through the cactus bush and parched the elm grove. Beyond the fringe was mountain laurel and beechnut spearmint, while over to the east were green moss-backed canoe-tops of lily-livered mountain lions, timber elks, moose, kiwanis, and neighborhood rotaries. I swam out into a pool of water. It felt good to swim out. I was reading a fine book, a story of a horse, and the boy who loved him.

Then Steve came back, and we took out the wine and

drank. He showed me his fish, and I showed him mine. He let me touch his fish, but I would not let him touch mine. We drank some more. The wine was icy cold, and tasted faintly rusty, so I drank it out of the bottle and followed each swallow with a chaser of chrome cleaner. Then, of course, the chrome cleaner reminded me of when I was in Africa hunting the big game. I thought about it. I had good thinking. I thought about the native boys we had in our group, who carried the guns and set up the camp and did everything while we drank and thought about the war. There was a guide in our party, a man named Williams. He had seen a lot of action in the jungle, and had been killed three times.

One morning we all awoke early. We knew we were going to hunt for very big game that day. We parked our gear and set off through the savanna. We hiked through the veldt and the steppes, and marched across the tundra and Tigris and the Euphrates. We passed many ferocious tigers and pumas that morning, but we were not out after them. We passed lions and zebras also, but we were not out after them either.

"We are not out after these poor brutes," Williams had told us. "You gents want to hunt the big game, or spend your time killing animals?"

We hiked along into the afternoon, and soon came to the place where, Williams said, the big game came to graze. I checked my rifle, and double-checked the pump barrel, safety catch, telescopic sight, barrel bore, and flintstone. Each chamber held a Schnauzer .414 shell. They were very powerful weapons. We hid in the tall grass, and in a while we heard the sound. There was a rustling of trees, and a shaking of dice and very large plastic pieces. Paper money began drifting down through the jungle growth. Williams squinted off into the distance.

"M'boomi m'boomi m'boomi boo?" asked one of the boys, a young tent carrier.

Williams shrugged and spat. "Can't tell, lad. Could be Rich Uncle. Sounds like Careers. Too early to tell."

Suddenly the wind shifted, and Williams leaped to his feet and cried, "There! See it? Careful, now . . . easy, gents. . . ." It was an enormous set of Monopoly, the largest I had ever seen. It came charging directly at us. The natives scattered. Two were knocked unconscious by huge green plastic houses that the Monopoly flung left and right. I saw Williams dodge a large die. Suddenly, the fear drained out of me, and I stood very still in the field and aimed the rifle and squeezed off the two rounds. The noise was very loud.

I saw the board lurch backward, and topple. Then came a rain of paper money, of many different colors. There were many twenties. Then the board fell, and was buried under its own money as more houses and big red hotels with good small rooms and warm beds fell around us. Then something hit me on the head, and I passed out. They told me later that it had been a falling deed, maybe one of the orange ones to New York or Tennessee. The camp was pretty much destroyed by the falling deeds, but we did not care. That night we had a great feast and roasted all the Chance and Community Chest cards over a bonfire and ate heartily.

It was a good memory. Damned good. But the sun was

setting, and Steve and I had to pack and get back to the town.

V

The next day the festival was really started. All over the town people were dancing and singing and having fun. We walked around the town and saw the signs: HURRAY FOR WINE! HURRAY FOR THE COCKS AND BULLS! YANQUIS GO JOME! "Let's go see the bulls," I said to the others.

We walked to a corral where the bulls were. Many men and boys were standing around the perimeter of the area. I saw a man whom I knew from many years of coming to San Cugat. His name was Marimba, and he owned a café. I walked over to him.

"Your friends, have they *afición?*" he asked.

"Some," I said. "Not as much as I do, though." He nodded.

Afición means passion. There are those who have it, and those who do not. The cock and bull fights are a special ritual in Spain and only those who have *afición* can truly appreciate the spectacle. Without *afición,* the fights are nothing. Those with *afición* know much about the *bullfighters* and the *cockfighters*, because bulls and cocks have *afición* also. Men like Marimba would forgive anything in a bull or a cock with *afición;* fear, nervousness, fibbing, incest, extortion, anything. Otherwise, though, it is nothing.

Soon, there was the running of the bulls. The gates to the corral were opened, and the bulls ran around the city.

Some of them went to good restaurants and ate *paella* and *bifstec*. Others just joined us at Marimba's café and got tight. Then we went to the cock house to watch the cocks warm up. There were many old bulls there, bulls too old or weak to be good bullfighters, but who were useful as practice partners for the young cocks. The cocks were dressed in their sweatsuits, each with the name of his sponsor sewn onto the back. JAIME'S LIQUORS, ROBERTO BAMA AUTO PARTS, JULIO MORON, REG. PLUMBER. The cocks hefted their weighted pics, and unsheathed their knives. Then they went at each other for a few practice rounds, not trying very hard to score any cuts since after all it was only practice.

"It is sad," Marimba said. He shook his head. "When I am a young man, there are many bulls and cocks and the fighting is good. Today, however . . . it is nothing. . . ."

After a few more drinks and a few more drinks we went to the arena. Steve was tight, and Bob was drunk, and I was cockeyed, and we had a good party. We sat in the sun and passed a bottle back and forth. We did this for an hour before we noticed that the bottle did not have any wine in it, and was empty.

"I say, Abe, we *are* enjoying ourselves," Steve said.

Then the procession started. First the judges and referees came out, wearing their long dark robes and striped shirts. Then there were musicians. The pipes and fifes were playing the *riau-riau* music, and the drums were making the boom-boom. Finally, the bulls came out, the large hump of muscle on their backs fitted with the cock-saddles. They marched out in a solemn procession, dressed in bright silks and deep red capes. Then came the cocks, carrying their special pics and holding at their sides the sheathed knives. They too marched slowly to the *riau-riau* boom-boom, and were very proud.

I sat beside Bob and explained to her what it was all about. We watched as the cocks mounted their bulls and settled into the saddle. Then Bob saw the cocks set with their pics, and unsheath the knives. The blades flashed in the sun, which was very hot on the yellowish sand. There were six cock-and-bull teams competing, and all over the arena the people were cheering on their favorite team. The six teams formed a circle in the center of the arena, and a referee stood in the middle with a yellow kerchief held aloft. There was a great silence. The flags around the arena hung limply in the heat. Steve passed me something to drink, but it was only chrome cleaner, so I didn't take much. Then the referee dropped the kerchief, and the fight began.

I explained to Bob that the object of the fight was for each cock to cut off the ears of the other bulls and finally to kill the other cocks with the pics. There were several rules that made the cock-and-bull fights a test of skill and courage, and not just a lot of animals running after each other. No cock could be killed until all bulls had their ears cut off. If any cock was killed before that time, he and his killer were eliminated, and the bulls also. Once all ears had been cut off, an umpire raised a green flag called an *andi-panda,* and then the work with the pics began. Any cock who fell off his bull was, of course, in great danger, as was any bull who lost his cock. There was great power in the partnership between the bull and the cock, and people with *afición* came from all over the world to see these fights.

It was becoming clear that the competition was mainly centering on two teams, with the other four barely keeping up. Already most ears had been cut, with the people in the stands crying *"Otro oido!"* every time another ear fell bloodily to the sand. Marimba was sitting next to Steve, and I saw him shake his head and say, "It is nothing." It was true, because most of the cocks were clumsy with the knives, and the ears were cut sloppily and without grace. Soon many people sensed this, and began throwing old pig's feet onto the area ground and calling abusive things to the animals. They ignored the crowd.

When all ears had been cut and the green flag raised, the air became more tense. Not long after that, the first cock was killed, and his bull had to carry him off on a stretcher assisted by an old steer who was the trainer. The cock-and-bull teams ran around the arena after each other, and the sun grew hotter. I told Bob not to look at the bulls when they got hit, but she could not take her eyes off them. After a while all cocks had been killed except two, and they stalked each other warily. The bulls were very tired, but they did not stop. They circled each other, the cocks lashing out with the pics. The crowd was silent. The sun was high in the sky, there was no shade for anyone.

The cocks soon tired. Their pics dropped, and they slouched in their saddles. Soon the bulls had slowed to a kind of shuffle, and it began to look as if the two teams were doing a slow cha-cha. The few remaining people with *afición* in the stands began to boo, then they too went to sleep. I looked over at Bob and Steve, and the three of us left the arena, picking our way past the sleeping bodies.

Just before we left I turned back to the arena and saw one of the cocks run his pic through the other one. Some people cheered, and a young girl skipped across the blood-caked sand and handed the victorious cock the key to the city.

VI

After that we went back to Paris. I ran into Jay Scott FitzDiver on the rue Genêt.

"Abe! Old sport!" He looked like hell.

"You look like hell," I said.

"Oh, I know it, old sport. How's the writing?"

"All right." That set me thinking. The writing, oh yes, I remembered when I was up in Michigan. Whenever I would be unable to write, I would go to the window and look out and think, "Do not worry. You have always written before. You can do it. You are a big boy now. Now go to the mirror." I would go to the mirror and look at myself. Then I would say, "Every day and in every way, I am getting better and better." Then I would think, "Now go write one true sentence," and I would sit down and write: The quick brown fox jumped over the lazy dog's back. Then I would go to a fine bar and drink anisette. I would dip my big toe in the dark green liquid until it turned a cloudy amber, and my big toe turned a deep orange. The writing of that one true sentence was easy, and a bad discipline. But the drinking of anisette was good.

"What are you doing, Jay?" I asked him.

"Oh, not much, old sport. I'm just traveling. A week or

two here, a week there. In about a month I thought I'd go back to the States, write some love stories for *McCall's,* go insane, and kill myself."

I said I thought it was a fine idea, and that was what he did. Meanwhile, I crossed the rue Bourée. By then it was night, and after a few drinks I went back to my hotel, took out the gun I had used to kill the big game, and cleaned it.

—*Ellis Weiner*

DEATH IN THE RUMBLE SEAT

▶ ▶ ▶ ▶ ▶ *M*ost people don't like the pedestrian part, and it is best not to look at that if you can help it. But if you can't help seeing them, long-legged and their faces white, and then the shock and the car lifting up a little on one side, then it is best to think of it as something very unimportant but beautiful and necessary artistically. It is unimportant because the people who are pedestrians are not very important, and if they were not being *cogido* by automobiles it would just be something else. And it is beautiful and necessary because, without the possibility of somebody getting *cogido*, driving a car would be just like anything else. It would be like reading "Thanatopsis," which is neither beautiful nor necessary, but hogwash. If you drive a car, and don't like the pedestrian part, then you are one of two kinds of people. Either you haven't very much vitality and you ought to do something about it, or else you are yellow and there is nothing to be done about it at all.

If you don't know anything about driving cars you are apt to think a driver is good just because he goes fast. This may be very exciting at first, but afterwards there is a bad taste in the mouth and the feeling of dishonesty. Ann

Bender, the American, drove as fast on the Merrick Road as anybody I have ever seen, but when cars came the other way she always worked out of their terrain and over in the ditch so that you never had the hard, clean feeling of danger, but only bumping up and down in the ditch, and sometimes hitting your head on the top of the car. Good drivers go fast too, but it is always down the middle of the road, so that cars coming the other way are dominated, and have to go in the ditch themselves. There are a great many ways of getting the effect of danger, such as staying in the middle of the road till the last minute and then swerving out of the pure line, but they are all tricks, and afterwards you know they were tricks, and there is nothing left but disgust.

The cook: I am a little tired of cars, sir. Do you know any stories?

I know a great many stories, but I'm not sure that they're suitable.

The cook: To hell with that.

Then I will tell you the story about God and Adam and naming the animals. You see, God was very tired after he got through making the world. He felt good about it, but he was tired as he asked Adam if he'd mind thinking up names for the animals.

"What animals?" Adam said.

"Those," God said.

"Do they have to have names?" Adam said.

"You've got a name, haven't you?" God said.

I could see——

The cook: How do *you* get into this?

Some people always write in the first person, and if you

do it's very hard to write any other way, even when it doesn't altogether fit into context. If you want to hear this story, don't keep interrupting.

The cook: O.K.

I could see that Adam thought God was crazy, but he didn't say anything. He went over to where the animals were, and after a while he came back with a list of names.

"Here you are," he said.

God read the list, and nodded.

"They're pretty good," he said. "They're all pretty good except that last one."

"That's a good name," Adam said. "What's the matter with it?"

"What do you want to call it an elephant for?" God said.

Adam looked at God.

"It looks like an elephant to me," he said.

The cook: Well?

That's all.

The cook: It is a very strange story, sir.

It is a strange world, and if a man and a woman love each other, that is strange too, and what is more, it always turns out badly.

In the golden age of car-driving, which was about 1910, the sense of impending disaster, which is a very lovely thing and almost nonexistent, was kept alive in a number of ways. For one thing, there was always real glass in the windshield so that if a driver hit anything, he was very definitely and beautifully *cogido*. The tires weren't much good either, and often they'd blow out before you'd gone ten miles. Really, the whole car was built that way. It was made not only so that it would precipitate accidents but so that when the accidents came it was honestly vulnerable, and it would fall apart, killing all the people with a passion that was very fine to watch. Then they began building the cars so that they would go much faster, but the glass and the tires were all made so that if anything happened it wasn't real danger, but only the false sense of it. You could do all kinds of things with the new cars, but it was no good because it was all planned in advance. Mickey Finn, the German, always worked very far into the other car's terrain so that the two cars always seemed to be one. Driving that way he often got the *faender,* or the clicking when two cars touch each other in passing, but because you knew that nothing was really at stake it was just an empty classicism, without any value because the insecurity was all gone and there was nothing left but a kind of mechanical agility. It is the same way when any art gets into its decadence. It is the same way about s–x——

The cook: I like it very much better when you talk about s–x, sir, and I wish you would do it more often.

I have talked a lot about s–x before, and now I thought I would talk about something else.

The cook: I think that is very unfortunate, sir, because you are at your best with s–x, but when you talk about automobiles, you are just a nuisance.

—*Wolcott Gibbs*

THE NOSE OF KILLER MANGIARO

▶ ▶ ▶ ▶ ▶ "*If* he don't show up soon, we'll go and get him."

The two fight managers had waited in the gym since early morning. Killer Mangiaro, a middleweight native of Florence, was supposed to tune up one last time for his fight with MacPherson in the public arena across the town.

"What time you got?"

"We have to get him."

"We might as well go now. Where do you suppose he is?"

They walked through the streets of Florence. "Fuh-rinzy," one of them said.

"Fee-renzy," the other corrected. "Fee-renzy Eetalia." They crossed the Ponte Vecchio over the Arno running through the streets of Florence. They were miserable. If their man was in a bar, he would be difficult to get out. It is a lot like handling a wounded bull. A bull that has been wounded will not be moved unless you approach him too quickly. Then he will charge you and gore you and kill you. So it is best to be gentle with a wounded bull. So it is best to be gentle with Killer Mangiaro.

He was seated in Harry's Bar. The two fight managers

saw him through the window. It was still early in the day. The bar did not seem crowded. "How's about you go in and talk to him, you see? You speak wop, don't you. You could calm him down.

"Sure. You wait out here. He don't like you."

"He don't like you either. But you baby him and he likes that. He don't like you either, you know."

"Sure I know." He walked inside the bar. His eyes adjusted to the light slowly. "Thou art a great and noble and renowned master of the boxing," he said to Mangiaro.

"I am tired," Mangiaro said.

"Thou hast the strength and the speed and the skill which God hath given thee. Come with me to the gymnasium and we will punch the heavy bag and skip the rope."

"I am tired."

"I know that. I know that thou art drained of thy strength."

"Not the weakness," said Mangiaro. "It is the fear. I am afraid. Another," he said quietly to the bartender.

"Always thou hast this fear."

"Always," agreed Mangiaro. "You know my fear and this Scotsman knows my fear also."

"MacPherson knows not of your fear."

"I am afraid." His glass arrived. "No, I shall not go back with thee this time." He raised the glass of bourbon to his lips and the manager punched him hard, once, between the eyes in the middle of his face. Mangiaro dropped the glass. His nostrils grew big, and his eyes unfocused and his hands dropped down to his sides and he slumped down on the bar.

"Geez Chrise," the other manager came running into the

bar. "You sucker punch him? He's not gonna like that. Geez Chrise."

"He don't like to get hit in the nose. You ever notice that? He don't like anybody to know he don't like to get hit in the nose either. He'll be all right when he comes to."

"You want me to help move him? Geez Chrise, right in the nose."

—Steven Goldleaf

JACK SPRAT

▶ ▶ ▶ ▶ ▶ "*C*ome in, Jack."

"I d'wanta come in."

"D'wanta come in, hell. Come in, bright boy."

They went in.

"I'll have eats now," she said. She was fat and red.

"I'd want nothing," Jack said. He was thin and pale.

"D'want nothin', hell. You have eats now, bright boy."

She called the waiter. "Bud," she said, "gimme bacon and beans—twice."

Bud brought the bacon and beans.

"I d'want bacon. It's too fat," Jack said.

"D'want bacon, hell. I'll eat the fat. You eat the lean. OK, big boy?"

"OK," Jack said.

They had eats.

"Now lick the plate clean," she said.

"Aw, honey," said Jack, "I aint gotta, do I?"

"Yup," she said. "You gotta."

They both licked their plates clean.

—*Henry Hetherington*